A BIBLIOGRAPHY OF PUBLISHING
AND THE BOOK CHAIN
IN SUB-SAHARAN AFRICA – 1996

PERSPECTIVES ON AFRICAN BOOK DEVELOPMENT

A BIBLIOGRAPHY OF PUBLISHING AND THE BOOK CHAIN IN SUB-SAHARAN AFRICA - 1996

(being a supplement to
*Publishing and Book Development
in Sub-Saharan Africa:
An Annotated Bibliography*)

HANS M. ZELL

WORKING GROUP
ON BOOKS AND LEARNING MATERIALS
ASSOCIATION FOR THE DEVELOPMENT OF EDUCATION IN AFRICA

British Library Cataloguing in Publication Data
Zell, Hans M. (Hans Martin), 1940-
   A bibliography of publishing and the book chain in Sub-Saharan Africa – 1996
   (Perspectives on African book development; v.3)
   1. Publishers and publishing – Africa, Sub-saharan – Bibliography
   2. Booksellers and bookselling – Africa, Sub-Saharan – Bibiography
   1. Title
   016'.0705'0967

Library of Congress Cataloguing in Publication Data
A catalogue record for this book has been requested

Published by Working Group on Books and Learning Materials
of the Association for the Development of Education in Africa
PO Box 2564, London W5 1ZD, United Kingdom

First published 1997

ISBN 1 901830 04 7

Distributed by ABC, African Books Collective Ltd., The Jam Factory,
27 Park End Street, Oxford OX1 1HU, United Kingdom
Tel: +44-(0) 1865-726686
Fax: +44-(0) 1865-793298
Email: abc@dial.pipex.com

Formatting and typesetting by Cécile Lomer
Production by Aldridge Press
24 Thorney Hedge Road, London W4 5SD
Cover Design: Geoffrey Wadsley

Printed and bound in Great Britain
by Antony Rowe Ltd., Chippenham, Wiltshire

CONTENTS

Contents

4 STUDIES BY TOPIC OR SUBJECT

Introduction

This bibliography on the 'book chain' in Sub-Saharan Africa is a supplement to *Publishing and Book Development in Sub-Saharan Africa: An Annotated Bibliography,* compiled and edited by Hans M. Zell & Cécile Lomer, and published by Hans Zell Publishers, an imprint of Bowker-Saur/Reed Reference Publishing in March 1996 (ISBN 1-873836-46-5). It is published with the financial support of the Association for the Development of Education in Africa (ADEA) Working Group on Books and Learning Materials, which is gratefully acknowledged.

It aims to provide a current awareness and quasi-abstracting service of the rapidly increasing literature on the various aspects of the 'book chain' in Africa. This is the first supplementary volume, covering 1996, and it is hoped that future 'supplements' or annual volumes can be published for 1997 and beyond.

Scope

The bibliography selectively records, annotates and classifies literature on the subject which has appeared since publication of the main bibliography cited above. For the most part this is literature published in 1996, but also included are a number of items published in late 1995, as well as some earlier references not previously listed, but which are now recorded. Late entries, published before 1995 or 1996, are indicated by the symbol <. However such late entries are restricted to books or articles published over the last ten years, i.e. since 1986. Any earlier material previously missed out will be included in a new edition of the main bibliography, and which may be published in a few year's time.

Whereas I have attempted to be as comprehensive as possible, I would be grateful to receive details of any articles or other documents that have escaped my attention - especially more elusive and difficult-to-track down articles published in Africa - in order to include them in future supplementary volumes to the main bibliography. (Please send any such material to me at PO Box 56, Oxford OX1 2SJ, UK. Fax: +44-1865-311534; Email: hzell@dial.pipex.com).

The bibliography covers new serials, books, reference sources, reports, papers in edited collections, periodical articles, as well as book sector studies and similar documents. Short reports, book reviews, and news items in *The African Book Publishing Record*, APNET's *African Publishing Review*, or short pieces which have appeared in the *Bellagio Publishing Network Newsletter* or elsewhere are not, for the most part, included. A select number of unpublished papers and documents (i.e. academic exercises, conference/seminar papers, consultant reports, etc.) have been included provided that copies can be made available to researchers. Some of these documents may however have restricted circulation.

Introduction

Material included

The bibliography aims to cover all segments of the book industries, book marketing and distribution, and the retail book trade on the continent. This includes the literature on more specialist areas of publishing, such as children's book publishing, scholarly publishing, or publishing in the African languages; and there are sections on complementary aspects of book development, such as authors and publishing, copyright, the reading habit and reading promotion, national book policies, and training for book industry personnel. Moreover, the bibliography covers the literature on a number of related topics, for example book assistance and donation programmes, the acquisition of African-published material, or publishing (in Africa and elsewhere) of African writers and African literature. Also included are articles on African journals and magazines, provided that such articles deal, at least in part, with publishing and/or distribution aspects of these journals.

However, there are some areas that are outside the scope of this bibliography, although it could be argued that they, too, are part of the 'book chain'. Literature on the following topics/subjects is *not* included: censorship, children's writing and literature (unless covering publishing aspects at least in part), librarianship and documentation, literacy, mass media and communication, newspaper publishing, and writing (e.g. developing writing skills, or report writing). Also, general articles on good practice in publishing, for example those appearing in the *African Publishing Review* or other African book trade journals, are not included.

Arrangement

Material listed is arranged in accordance with the special subject heading authority and classification system that has been established for the database of the main bibliography.

As a general rule, most articles on particular topics or areas of the book trade are classified under *topic* as the primary heading, but are indexed both by topic and by country or region. Books and articles which primarily deal with publishing and the state of the book in a particular country or region are classified under country or region as the primary heading. However, national book sector studies, or articles on national book policies in different African countries, are all grouped under the section 'National book policies', though also indexed by country.

Under many subject/topic headings 'see also' references guide the user to related topics, and there are also a number of cross-references to items listed in the main bibliography.

2

Entries/Annotations

Complete bibliographical data is provided for each entry. Entries are numbered consecutively starting with entry 2268, as a continuation of the main bibliography. Most of the material has been personally examined by the compiler, and annotations or abstracts are provided for most entries. I have attempted to provide *informative* annotations, but they tend to be descriptive rather than critical. However, the absence of an annotation should not be taken as implying the work or the article has less value than annotated entries, as in some cases I was unable to examine a copy of the article or document.

Periodicals cited in the bibliography

For a complete list of periodicals cited (and their place of publication) see the main bibliography pp.7-15.

The following periodicals are *new* to the list and have not been previously cited.

ADEA Newsletter [Association for the Development of Education in Africa] (Paris)
African Association of Science Editors Newsbrief-Ethiopian Chapter (Addis Ababa)
AfriquEducation (Montrouge, France)
Author, The (London)
BDC Export News [Book Development Council] (London)
Bukku (Conakry)
CASP News Digest [Consortium for African Scholarly Publishing] (Nairobi)
Catholic Media Council Information Bulletin (Aachen, Germany)
Collection Building (New York)
D&C (Bonn)
Development in Practice (Oxford)
ERA Initiative, The (Yeoville, South Africa)
Ghana Book News (Accra)
Journal of Scholarly Publishing (Toronto) [formerly Scholarly Publishing]
Le Livre Africain (Cotonou)
Mohlomi (Roma, Lesotho)
NGAO Newsletter [Network for the Defence of Independent Media in Africa]
  (Nairobi)
Orbit (Lusaka)
Scientific American (New York)
South African Children's Book Forum (Grabouw, South Africa)
Uganda Book News (Kampala)
Whydah (Nairobi)
Writers World (Somerset West, South Africa)

Indexes

An author and a subject/geographical index is included. References are to item numbers.

Directory of organizations

A short directory of the principal organizations involved in, and/or supporting publishing and book development in Africa precedes the bibliography section. For a fuller listing of organizations (including African book trade associations, African book development councils, etc.) refer to the main bibliography, pp. 16-29.

Acknowledgements

For drawing my attention to a number of articles and other documents which might have escaped my attention I am grateful to Philip Altbach and Damtew Teferra of the Bellagio Publishing Network Research and Information Center, Mary Jay of African Books Collective Ltd., Carol Priestley of ADEA, Katherine Salahi of the Bellagio Publishing Network Secretariat, and Kelvin Smith of CODE Europe.

HMZ

April 1997

Directory of Organizations and Networks

This directory lists some of the organizations and networks listed in the bibliography (or from whom unpublished documents are available). For a much fuller listing of organizations involved in, or supporting, publishing and the 'book chain' in Africa, including names and addresses of national book trade associations or book development councils, see the directory in the main bibliography, pp. 16-29.

African Association of Science Editors (AASE)
c/o Addis Ababa University Research and Publications Office
PO Box 1176
Addis Ababa
Ethiopia
Tel: +251-1-114323/111514 Fax: +251-1-552350
Email: sue@padis.gn.apc.org

African Books Collective Ltd. (ABC)
The Jam Factory
27 Park End Street
Oxford OX1 1HU
UK
Tel: +44(0)1865-726686 Fax: +44(0)1865-793298
Email: abc@dial.pipex.com
Website: http://www.sas.upenn.edu/African_Studies/Publications/ABC_Menu.html

African Publishers Network (APNET)
11th Floor Megawatt House
44 Samora Machel Avenue
PO Box 3773
Harare
Zimbabwe
Tel: +263-4-706196/7 Fax: +263-4-705106
Email: apnet@mango.apc.org

Afro-Asian Book Council (AABC)
4835/24 Ansari Road
Darya Ganji
New Delhi 110002
India
Tel: +91-11-326 1487 Fax: +91-1-326 7437

Agence de la Francophonie (ACCT)
(Programme: 'Edition scolaire du Sud')
Ecole Internationale de la Francophonie
15-16 quai Louis XVIII
3300 Bordeaux
France
Tel: +33-5-56 01 59 00 Fax: +33-5-56 51 78 20
Email: eif@Francophonie.org
Website: http://www.Francophonie.org

Association for the Development of Education in Africa (ADEA)
International Institute for Educational Planning
7-9 rue Eugène-Delacroix
75116 Paris
France
Tel: +33-1-45 03 37 96 Fax: +33-1-45 03 39 65
Email: adea@iiep.unesco.org

ADEA Working Group on Books and Learning Materials
Working Group Convener: Carew Treffgarne
Department for International Development
94 Victoria Street
London SW1E 5JL
UK
Tel: +44(0)171-917 0658 Fax: +44(0)171-917 0287
Email: c-treffgarne@dfid.gtnet.gov.uk

Working Group Coordinator: Carol Priestley
PO Box 2564
London W5 1ZD
UK
Tel: +44(0)181-997 3274 Fax: +44(0)181-810 9795
Email: cpriestley@gn.apc.org

Bellagio Publishing Network
Oxford Secretariat:
The Jam Factory
27 Park End Street
Oxford OX1 1HU
UK
Tel: +44(0)1865-794068 Fax: +44(0)-1865-244584
Email: bellpubnet@gn.apc.org

Research and Information Center:
School of Education
Boston College
Chestnut Hill
MA 02167
USA
Tel: +1-617-552 4236 Fax: +1-617-552 8422
Email: Altbach@bc.edu
Website: http://www.bc.edu/bc_org/avp/soe/cihe/bell.html

CODE Europe
Partners in African Publishing
The Jam Factory
27 Park End Street
Oxford
OX1 1HU
UK
Tel: +44(0)1865 202438 Fax: +44(0)1865-202439
Email: 100660.2023@compuserve.com
Website: http:/www.oneworld.org/code_europe

Consortium for African Scholarly Publishing (CASP)
c/o African Centre for Technology Studies
PO Box 45917
Nairobi
Kenya
Tel: +254-2-565173   Fax: +254-2-569989
Email: acts@arso.sasa.unon.org

Council for the Promotion of Children's Science Publishing in Africa (CHISCI)
PO Box 61301
Nairobi
Kenya
Tel: +254-2-442341   Fax: +254-2-564376

International Network for the Availability of Scientific Publications (INASP)
PO Box 2564
London W5 1ZD
UK
Tel: +44(0)181-997 3274 Fax: +44(0)181-810 9795
Email: inasp@gn.apc.org
Website: http://www.oneworld.org/inasp/index.html

Network of Technical Publications in Africa (TEPUSA)
Plot no. 28/18616 Morogoro Road
PO Box 20986
Dar es Salaam
Tanzania

Pan African Booksellers Association (PABA)
c/o Booksellers Association of Zimbabwe
New Book House
78 Kaguvi Street
PO Box 3916
Harare
Zimbabwe
Tel: +263-4-751202

Southern African Book Development Education Trust
25 Endymion Road
London N4 1EE
UK
Tel: +44(0)181-348 8463 Fax: +44(0)181-348 4403
Email: margaret.ling@geo2.poptel.org.uk

United Nations Educational, Scientific and Cultural Organization (UNESCO)
Book & Cultural Industries Section (CLT/CIC/BCI) [formerly Book & Copyright Division]
1 rue Miollis
75732 Paris
France
Tel: +33-1-45 68 47 10 Fax: +33-1-45 68 55 95
Email: a.garzon@unesco.org

Zimbabwe International Book Fair Trust
PO Box CY 1179
Causeway
Harare
Zimbabwe
Tel: +263-4-702104/702108 Fax: +263-4-702129
Email: zibf@samara.co.zw
Website: http://www.mediazw.com/zibf/

1 Serials/Reference/Biography/Handbooks and teaching guides

Serials

2268

< *African Association of Science Editors Newsbrief (Ethiopian Chapter).* Volume 1, no. 1, 1993- Irregular. Edited by Damtew Teferra. Addis Ababa: African Association of Science Editors [PO Box 30231].

> Reports about the activities of the African Association of Science Editors (AASE), and provides a variety of tips and suggestions for good practice in scientific publishing.

2269

Bukku. Publier en Langues Nationales. Bulletin de liaison des professionnels du livre en Afrique. Number 1, April 1996- Irregular. Edited by Mamadou Aliou Sow. Conakry: Editions Ganndal [BP 542].

> Bukku (which means 'book' in several African languages) is a newsletter for book professionals in Africa who are involved in the publication, promotion, and distribution of African language publications in various parts of the continent. Contains news about African language publishing activities, and reports about various new initiatives. Published with the financial support of the German Foundation for International Development.

2270

CASP News Digest. Volume 1, no. 1, April 1996- Quarterly. Edited by Elizabeth Larson. Nairobi: Consortium for African Scholarly Publishing (CASP), African Centre for Technology Studies

> Includes reports about CASP activities, meetings and workshops held, and short articles on various aspects of scholarly publishing.

2271

The ERA Initiative. [not numbered], 1995[?]- Annual[?]. Edited by Beulah Thumbadoo. Yeoville, South Africa: Easy Reading for Adults (ERA) [43 Harley Street, Yeoville 2198, PO Box 501, Wits 2050].

> Newsletter of an organization that seeks to build a reading environment by supporting the production and dissemination of easy reading materials for adults, particularly in the African languages.

2272

Le Livre Africain. Le Journal de la Culture, de l'Education & du Développement. Volume 1, no. 1, 1975- Quarterly. Edited by Bertin Fondjo. Cotonou: Intermonde SARL [01 BP 327 Recette Principale].

> New quarterly journal that aims to promote the book industries in Africa, as well as promoting educational and cultural development. Contains news items, short feature

articles, poetry, book reviews, etc. The journal's publisher also sponsors an annual book fair and a book prize (Prix Giacomo Leopardi) for children and young adults.

2273

South African Children's Book Forum. [not numbered], 1996[?]-. Edited by Jay Heale. Grabouw, South Africa: South African section of IBBY [PO Box 541, 7160 Grabouw].

A four-page newsletter of IBBY's South African section, with short news items about children's book activities in South Africa. The issue examined also reports that Bookchat, edited by Jay Heale (see main bibliography, item 9), will cease publication at the end of 1997, but that some of the magazine's features may be transferred to this newsletter.

2274

Uganda Book News. Volume 1, no. 1, January/March 1996- Quarterly. Edited by Martin Okia. Kampala: Uganda Publishers and Booksellers Association (UPABA) [PO Box 7732].

The official publication of the Uganda Publishers and Bookseller Association. Contains notes and news about the activities of the Association, and short articles about publishing and library development in Uganda.

Bibliographies

2275

Africa Book Centre *The Africa Book Centre Book Review.* London: Africa Book Centre Ltd. [38 King Street, London WC2E 8JT]. no. 1, 1995- Quarterly

Contains a small number of book reviews or review essays of books on certain topics/countries, occasional interviews, plus two separate annotated listings (lacking names of publishers) 'New Books from Africa' and 'New Books on Africa' arranged under broad subject groups.

2276

African Books Collective Ltd. *Complete Stock List, as at August 1995.* Oxford: African Books Collective Ltd., 1995, 95 pp.

ABC's first complete stock list of some 1,500 titles, distributed on behalf of 48 publishers in 14 African countries. Provides full bibliographic details and acquisitions data, arranged under 54 subject headings.

2277

African Books Collective Ltd. *Complete Stock List, as at November 1996.* Oxford: African Books Collective Ltd., 1996, 93 pp.

An update of the preceding entry, now including over 1,700 titles, from 50 African publishers.

2278

Internationale Jugendbibliothek *Jambo-Hello-Bonjour. Kinderliteratur aus und über Afrika*. Munich: Internationale Jugendbibliothek [Schloss Blutenburg, D-81247 Munich], 1996, 10 pp.

> Annotated catalogue of some 80 mostly African-published children's books which formed part of an exhibition held in Munich between March and May 1996.

2279

Association of Namibian Publishers *Namibian Books in Print 1996/1997. A catalogue of books from Namibia available through the book trade. Including the Namibian book world directory*. Compiled by Werner Hillebrecht. Windhoek: Association of Namibian Publishers [PO Box 5934, Ausspannplatz] 2nd ed., 1996. 131 pp.

> Second edition of Namibian Books in Print, now listing over 1,300 titles in print as at 1996 and providing very full bibliographic and acquisitions data. Arrangement is alphabetical by author, with co-author, title, subject, and language indexes. Also includes a listing of Namibian serial publications, plus a directory section: ISBN directory, Namibian publishers directory, Namibian book trade directory (i.e. bookshops and retail outlets), and a directory of organizations in the book and information sector.

2280

Nigerian Publishers Association *Nigerian Books in Print 1996*. Ibadan: Nigerian Publishers Association [PO Box 2541], 1996, 456 pp. (distributed outside Africa by African Books Collective Ltd., Oxford)

> The first publication of a Nigerian books in print listing for over 20 years (see also main bibliography, item 65). Contains some 5,000 entries from 65 Nigerian publishers, grouped in four sections: (i) pre-primary/primary, (ii) secondary, (iii) tertiary/research publications, and (iv) general. Arranged alphabetically by broad subject divisions, and each section has an author index. Nigerian publishers' names and addresses are provided in two sequences: members of the NPA, and non-members.

2281

Zell, Hans M., and Cécile Lomer *Publishing and Book Development in Sub-Saharan Africa: an annotated bibliography*. London: Hans Zell Publishers, an imprint of Bowker-Saur/Reed Reference Publishing, 1996, 424 pp.

> The main bibliography to which this present volume serves as a supplement. Contains 2,267 entries covering books, serials, reference sources, reports, papers in edited collections, book sector studies and similar documents, and periodical articles drawn from literature published in over 360 journals and magazines. Most entries are annotated, and thus provide a synthesis of past and current thinking on the growth and development of publishing in Africa. Also includes a directory of African book trade associations, and other organizations and networks supporting African publishing and book development. Extensively cross-referenced and indexed by author, subject and by country or region.

11

2282

Zell, Hans. M. "Publishing and Book Development in Sub-Saharan Africa 1995: a checklist of recent literature." *Bellagio Publishing Network Newsletter*, no. 17 (July 1996): 1-18 [separately paged].

> This annual checklist and (partial) update to the preceding entry is now superseded by the present bibliography.

Directories and other reference sources

2283

African Books Collective Ltd. *African Publishers Networking Directory 1997/98.* Oxford: African Books Collective Ltd., 1996 [copyright 1997], 54 pp. (Available gratis to the African book professions; others/outside Africa: £18/$30)

> A much expanded and fully updated version of a directory first published in 1993 (see main bibliography, item 95). Provides detailed information on some 360 major and/or most active publishers in Africa today: full names and addresses, telephone and fax numbers (and Email where available), year founded, ISBN prefix, name of chief executive, rights contact, number of titles in print and average number of new books published annually, nature of publisher's list, area(s) of specialization, and overseas distributors. Other listings include African book trade organizations, African book trade journals, and reference sources.

2284

Publishers' Association of South Africa *Publishers' Association of South Africa. Frankfurt 1996.*
Cape Town: Publishers' Association of South Africa [PO Box 116, St. James, 7946 Cape Town], 1996, 30 pp.

> Company profiles of 24 South African publishers who exhibited at the Frankfurt Book Fair in 1996. Also includes publishers' addresses, telephone and fax numbers, Email, names of key personnel, and details of number of titles published annually.

2285

Roberts, Frances *A Writer's Guide to South African Magazines.* Somerset West, South Africa: Options Publishing, 1996, 117 pp.

> Provides practical guidelines for freelance writers who wish to tap into the opportunities for publishing outlets offered by a variety of South African magazines. Each listing contains an analysis of a sample copy of the individual title (type of features and material accepted for publication, regular columns, payment offered, guidelines for contributors, etc.) together with full name and address, telephone and fax numbers (and Email for some), name of editor, frequency, format, average page extent per issue, and advertising content.

2286

Zimbabwe International Book Fair Trust/Southern African Book Development Education Trust *African Periodicals Exhibit Catalogue 1996.* Harare: Zimbabwe International Book Fair Trust; London: Southern African Book Development

Education Trust, 1996, 52 pp. (Available free-of-charge from SABDET, 25 Endymion Road, London N4 1EE)

A catalogue of over 100 African-published serials displayed at a collective exhibit at the 1996 Zimbabwe International Book Fair (for catalogues of previous exhibits see main bibliography, items 122-124). Provides full acquisitions data for each journal as well as descriptive annotation on contents. Includes an introductory essay by Hans M. Zell "African Journals in a Changing Environment of Scholarly Communication". (see entry 2489).

Indexes and indexing services

2287

Oshunfowora, Ranti E. *25 Years of Library, Archives, Publishing and Information Science Research: Index/abstracts of articles in selected Nigerian journals and books (1972-1996)*. Ibadan: Options Book and Information Services [Box 21259, University Post Office, University of Ibadan], 1996. 2 vols.

Indexes and abstracts seven Nigerian journal titles and includes 311 entries. (Not examined)

Biography & autobiography

2288

Hasan, Abul "Asanga Machwe is no More." *AABC Newsletter* 5, nos. 2/3 (July & October 1996): 3.

An obituary of the late Asanga Machwe, founder and former Secretary-General of the Afro-Asian Book Council (and Managing Director of New Age International Publishers), with a number of tributes by colleagues from Asia, Africa, and elsewhere.

2289

Pugliese, Cristiana *Author, Publisher and Gikuyu Nationalist: the life and writings of Gakaara wa Wanjau.* Bayreuth, Germany: Universität Bayreuth (Bayreuth African Studies Series, 37), 1995, 240 pp.

Biography of this Kenyan writer and publisher, who was the joint winner, in 1984, of the Noma Award for Publishing in Africa.

Handbooks for writers

2290

van Rooyen, Basil *How to Get Published in South Africa. A Guide for Authors.* Halfway House, South Africa: Southern Book Publishers, 2nd ed. 1996, 254 pp.

A new and updated edition of a practical hands-on guide for prospective authors, providing detailed tips and instructions how to find the right publisher, how to prepare a manuscript, etc. (see also main bibliography, entry 145, for first edition details). In this second edition chapters have been added on literary and children's book publishing, self-publishing, and publishing in African languages (see also entries 2368 and 2456) and the 'Directory of South African Publishers' at the back of the book has been substantially expanded.

Teaching guides and texts

→ **See also: Educational and school book publishing**

→ **Note:** This section only includes handbooks or teaching guides specifically designed either for use in Africa, and/or particularly relevant for use in developing countries.

2291

Châtry-Komarek, Marie *Tailor-Made Textbooks. A Practical Guide for the Authors of Textbooks in Primary Schools in Developing Countries.* Translated from the French. Oxford: CODE Europe, in association with the Deutsche Stiftung für internationale Entwicklung, 1996, 224 pp.
[Originally published in 1994 as *Des Manuels Scolaires sur Mesure: guide pratique à l'intention des auteurs de manuels scolaires pour le primaire dans les pays en développement*]

> A handbook for all those involved in the writing and production of textbooks in developing countries, though primarily intended as a tool and practical guide to assist textbook authors. It includes detailed, step-by-step descriptions of how to produce a textbook, covering all aspects of planning and preliminary research, development, illustrations, design and format, typography, artwork, page make up, as well as reviewing aspects of costs. There is also an appendix of project evaluations, a bibliography, and a helpful glossary of terms.

2292

Hall, John (Programme Manager), Etienne Brunswic, and Jean Valérien *Planning the Development of School Textbooks. A Series of Twelve Training Modules for Educational Planners and Administrators.* Paris: International Institute of Educational Planning, [7-9 rue Eugène-Delacroix, 75116 Paris], 1995. boxed set with 12 separate modules, separate Introduction/Instructions booklet, and Trainer's guide; var. pp., plus spreadsheets disk for Module 3.

> Designed for guided self-instruction, these twelve modules are intended both for planners - especially those working in central units of the Ministry of Education - and for administrators involved in the development of textbooks at its various stages: financing strategies, costing/programming, design, production, quality control, distribution and use, as well as management of the publishing process. Module 8 provides an introduction to desktop publishing. The modules "propose a methodology which should enable the participants to analyze a situation at any given time and to identify specific solutions to propose to decision-makers." A Trainer's Guide is included, as is a simulation model (on diskette) for Module 3: Quantifying Needs

2   General, Comparative, and Regional Studies

Comparative studies (General/comparative studies on publishing in developing countries)

2293

Garzón, Alvaro "The International 'Free Flow' of Books." [Unpublished, photocopy; available from UNESCO, Book and Copyright Division, Paris; 1996, 6 pp.]

Paper presented to the Interregional Meeting of Book Promotion Networks/ INTERBOOK, Paris, May 22-24, 1996. The Chief of UNESCO's book division reviews the principal agreements aiding the free flow of books and the UNESCO members states that are parties to these agreements: The Florence Agreement (and Nairobi Protocol), other regional agreements, and the General Agreement on Tariffs and Trade (GATT), which later became the World Trade Organization (WTO).

2294

International Book Development Ltd./International Federation of Library Associations. *Key Policy Issues in International Book, Library and Information Development. An IBD/IFLA seminar on policy development for aid agencies, policy planners, librarians, publishers and information suppliers, Imperial Hotel, Harrogate, 12-13 July 1995.* London, IBD Ltd. & Boston Spa: IFLA Offices for UAP and International Lending, c/o The British Library [Boston Spa, Wetherby, LS23 7BQ], 1995, [Unpublished, var. pp.]

A collection of 11 papers presented at a meeting which brought together a number book and information specialists with a particular interest in the developing world, and which examined the fundamental problems and issues of sustainable and adequate book and information provision.

2295

McCartney, Murray *Books for Millions. A seminar on low-cost and affordable book production and distribution, Harare, 30 July 1995.* New Delhi: Afro-Asian Book Council [4835/24 Ansari Road, New Delhi 110002], 1996, 16 pp.

Summary report about a one-day seminar jointly organized by APNET and the Afro-Asian Book Council, with summaries of the papers, the seminar conclusions and recommendations, and a list of delegates.

2296

Randle, Ian   "Publishing in the Caribbean. Trends and developments." *Bellagio Publishing Network Newsletter*, no. 17 (July 1996): 14-16.
[Also published in *IASP Newsletter*, no. 3 (1996): 3-5.]

Surveys the development of local book industries in the Caribbean, and examines the historical, cultural, and environmental contexts in which publishers struggle to operate, coupled with problems of undercapitalization, costly financing, unstable currencies, and government policies that serve as a disincentive to a flourishing indigenous book industry.

Emphasizes the need for the establishment of national book policies, and calls for the establishment of publishers associations and book development councils to help influence government policies towards the book trade, and which will be able to give direction to the growth of genuine indigenous publishing companies sensitive to local and regional needs.

Africa (General studies)

2297

Altbach, Philip G. "Bellagio Seminar Focuses on Trends in Privatization in African Publishing." *Bellagio Publishing Network Newsletter*, no. 17 (July 1996): 3-4.
> Report about a Bellagio Group-sponsored seminar, held in Copenhagen, Denmark, on June 18 and 19, 1996, on issues relating to the privatization of publishing in Africa.

2298

Altbach, Philip G. "Perspectives on Privatization in African Publishing." In *The Challenge of the Market: privatization and publishing in Africa*, edited by Philip G. Altbach. Chestnut Hill, MA: Bellagio Publishing Network, Research and Information Center (Bellagio Studies in Publishing, 7), 1996, 3-8.
[Also published in *Bellagio Publishing Network Newsletter*, no. 17 (July 1996): 16-18; also in *The Bookseller* as "A Fair Climate in Africa", no. 4726 (1996): 26-27; and in *West Africa* as "Publishing in Africa", no. 4123 (1996): 1711-1712.]
> State publishing in Africa, a powerful ideological force in the 1960s, has by and large failed to deliver, and state-run publishers have exhibited a combination of negative characteristics. Indigenous publishing does not have deep roots in Africa, and circumstances during the colonial era and its aftermath did not favour it. However, indigenous private sector publishing is now seeking to prove itself as a desirable alternative to state publishing, although it faces some daunting challenges and problems. The article reviews some of these elements - public policy, freedom to publish, access to credit, market size, competition with the multinationals, the World Bank and the Bank's textbook programmes, and intra-African book trade - which the author believes are central to providing a context, and to understanding the potential for successful private-sector publishing in Africa.

2299

Anon. "The Future of Indigenous Publishing in Africa-'Arusha II'." *The African Book Publishing Record* 22, no. 4 (1996): 181-182.
> Extracts from the summary conclusions of a Dag Hammarskjöld Foundation-sponsored seminar on 'The Future of Indigenous Publishing in Africa', held in Arusha, Tanzania, 25-28 March, 1995. (See also entry 2306)

2300

"Asang Machwe and the Low-cost Book." *African Publishing Review* 4, no. 6 (November/December 1995): 15-16.
> The late Asang Machwe, former Secretary General of the Afro-Asian Book Council and Managing Director of New Age International Publishers, talks to Lesley Humphrey,

editor of *African Publishing Review*, about the possibilities of low-cost publishing in Africa.

2301

Bgoya, Walter "Publishing in Africa: culture and development." In *The Muse of Modernity: essays on culture as development in Africa*, edited by Philip G. Altbach and Salah M. Hassan. Trenton, NJ: Africa World Press, 1996, 151-179.
[Revised entry, substitutes 'forthcoming' entry in main bibliography, item 239]

A wide-ranging essay examining the state of the African publishing industry "which is cast in a special position of privilege and disadvantage." Starts off with a broad overview of publishing in Africa, and then analyses textbook publishing as a tool for the promotion of culture, liberation history as a special publishing project, and the factors influencing the growth of the indigenous book industries, such as curricula, market size, the colonial legacy, and language issues. It also examines the role played by recent collaborative initiatives such as African Books Collective and the African Publishers' Network, book fairs, copyright issues and, in a final section, the author discusses the prospects for publishing of African creative writing, and journals publishing. In his conclusion the author argues that "cultural publishing deserves just as much attention as educational publishing", and that "publishing in African languages should be given first priority, so that as many people as possible may encounter the adventures of living that are found in fiction, poetry, and drama."

2302

Bgoya, Walter "Development and Future of Indigenous Publishing in Africa: 12 years after Arusha I." [Unpublished, photocopy; available from Dag Hammarskjöld Foundation, Uppsala, 1996, 30 pp.]

A scene-setting keynote paper presented to the second Dag Hammarskjöld Foundation seminar on publishing in Africa, Arusha, Tanzania, March 25-28, 1996. (see also entry 2306). Sets out to review what transpired in the twelve years after the first Dag Hammarskjöld Foundation Seminar on Development of Autonomous Publishing Capacity in Africa, which was held in Arusha in April 1984. It summarizes the broad consensus of participants in the 1984 seminar on the African publishing situation as it existed then, and the recommendations that emerged from the meeting. It then examines developments since 1984 and poses a number of questions "leading to determination of whether autonomous publishing capacity in Africa has been enhanced or not; what can and should be done to improve the situation so as to make African publishing not only viable commercially, but to make it also respond to the needs of a liberating education and culture as the 20th century comes to a close." An appendix includes a possible 'Framework for establishing equitable and mutually beneficial joint ventures in publishing in Africa.'

2303

Brickhill, Paul "The Transition from State to Commercial Publishing Systems in African Countries." In *The Challenge of the Market: privatization and publishing in Africa*, edited by Philip G. Altbach. Chestnut Hill, MA: Bellagio Publishing Network Research and Information Center (Bellagio Studies in Publishing, 7), 1996, 9-28.

Offers some insights into the problems and issues in the transition from state to private sector publishing now underway in several African countries. Based on studies undertaken in Tanzania, Zambia and Malawi, and observations and discussions with publishers from elsewhere. Sets out the background to state intervention in the book sector and analyses some of the effects of state control in publishing, its advantages and its critical weaknesses. While welcoming the transition to commercialization, the author identifies some flaws in some approaches to textbook provision by the private sector and states that there "is the apparent failure to recognize that the commercial sector must provide the impetus for change and demonstrate the technical proficiency required for textbook provision"; and that the commercial systems requires genuine competition among publishers, rather than being dominated by one or two, and without which it is likely to suffer many of the shortcomings of the previous state monopolies. The author also argues forcefully that a liberalized system of textbook supply must include all those who are part of the 'book chain', including booksellers and the retail book trade, and that Ministry of Education officials should not assume the role of booksellers, or attempting to manage book distribution systems.

2304

Chakava, Henry "The Missing Links in the African Book Publishing Chain" *Link-up* 8, no. 2 (June 1996): 20-26
Reprint of a paper which appeared in Promoting Technical Publishing in Africa. Seminar Proceedings, Arnhem, Netherlands, 3-6 November 1992. Wageningen, Netherlands: Technical Centre for Agricultural and rural Co-operation of ACP-EU (CTA), 1994 (for abstract see main bibliography, entry 252).

2305

Chakava, Henry *Publishing in Africa: one man's perspective.* Chestnut Hill, MA: Bellagio Publishing Network Research and Information Centre (Bellagio Studies in Publishing, 6); Nairobi: East African Educational Publishers, 1996, 182 pp.
A collection of essays and articles by one of Africa's most prolific commentators on the African publishing scene, bringing together his writings on many diverse topics, such as autonomous publishing, book marketing and distribution, author-publisher relations, regional cooperation, the World Bank and African publishing, reading promotion, the inequalities of international copyright, and the problems of censorship and government repression. Most of the articles have previously appeared in edited collections and/or in various academic and professional journals (see main bibliography, various entries). Also contains one entirely new paper, "Book Marketing and Distribution: The Achilles Heel of African Publishing" (see entry 2442).

2306

Davies, Wendy *The Future of Indigenous Publishing in Africa. A seminar organized by the Dag Hammarskjöld Foundation in Arusha, Tanzania, March 25-28, 1996. Seminar Report.* Uppsala: Dag Hammarskjöld Foundation [Ovre Slottsgatan 2, SE-75310 Uppsala], 1996, 32 pp.
A report about a Dag Hammarskjöld Foundation-sponsored seminar, which brought together 30 participants from eight countries, including publishers, writers, librarians, academics, and bankers. The report summarizes developments in indigenous African publishing since 1984 (when the DHF organized an earlier seminar on 'The Development of Autonomous Publishing Capacity in Africa'), and thereafter identifies the key issues that emerged from the papers presented and from the discussions: publishing as a strategic industry, reading and cultural environment, national book policy, communication and

networking, the electronic revolution, marketing and distribution, and finance. Also includes a summary of the conclusions, and a list of participants.

2307

< Frommelt, Wolfram "Books-First Victims of the Crisis." *D&C [Development & Coopération]*, no. 3 (1992): 24-26.

English version of German item listed in main bibliography, entry 276. Describes the book crisis in Africa--societies without books and without printed literature, and in danger of relapsing into illiteracy.

2308

Gedin, Per I. "A Real Cultural Revolution." [Unpublished, photocopy; available from Dag Hammarskjöld Foundation, Uppsala, 1996, 6 pp.]

Paper presented to the second Dag Hammarskjöld Foundation seminar on publishing in Africa, Arusha, Tanzania, March 25-28, 1996. Looks back on what has been achieved, and what has not been achieved, since the previous Dag Hammarskjöld Seminar held in Arusha in 1984 and areas of weaknesses which remain. Also describes innovations in printing technology, the 'electronic revolution', and digital presses, and the likely impact this will have on the publishing industry in Africa.

2309

Lema, Elieshi "The Future of African Indigenous Publisher: report of the Arusha seminar." *Bellagio Publishing Network Newsletter*, no. 17 (July 1996): 4-6.

Report about the presentations made at the Dag Hammarskjöld Foundation's 'Arusha II' seminar (see also entry 2308 above).

2310

Newton, Diana "Bridging the Anglophone-Francophone Divide." *Bellagio Publishing Network Newsletter*, no. 15 (August 1995): 11-12.

Argues that, when it comes to book publishing in Africa, "the English-French linguistic divide has created two distinct communities, with severely limited interaction between the two", and that "both sides will need to establish and maintain mechanisms for effective and timely information sharing that reach beyond isolated actions and token bilingualism." Recommends a number of activities that could be undertaken on the anglophone side to improve the situation.

2311

Philipparts, Michel "A Continent in Search of Publishers." *Catholic Media Council. Information Bulletin*, no. 1 (1996): 1-6

An overview of the current state of publishing in Africa, reviewing the major problems facing the book industries, and the role of the church and church publishers in book development. Includes some statistics of the number of publishers in Africa: secular, Catholic, and Protestant. Also reports about the establishment of the Association of Catholic Publishers in Africa, based in Nairobi.

2312

Zeleza, Paul "A Social Contract for Books." *The African Book Publishing Record* 22, no. 4 (1996): 251-255.

[Also published in *National Book Policies for Africa. The key to long-term development. Proceedings of the Zimbabwe International Book Fair Indaba 96, Harare, Zimbabwe, 26-27 July 1996*, edited by Murray McCartney. Harare: Zimbabwe International Book Fair Trust, 1996, 12-20; see entry 2501]

A slightly edited version of a keynote speech delivered by Paul Zeleza (winner of the 1994 Noma Award for Publishing in Africa) at an 'Indaba' on national book policies. It focuses, first, on the political and cultural economies of the African book industry, and, secondly, the social contract which the author believes needs to be forged between the six stakeholders he identifies, namely African governments, publishers, writers, educational institutions, libraries, and the general reading public. The author argues that a social contract for books, for the development of a vigorous reading culture and a flourishing indigenous book industry, requires specific commitments and tangible contributions from each of the stakeholders. He sets out what these requirements are, and concludes "Culture and books are too serious to be left to sympathetic foreigners or governments. All of us have a stake in them, for they embody our values, practices and possibilities, dreams and destiny, pasts and futures, our investment in a reflective, critical, and tolerant humanity."

Africa, East (Regional studies)

→ **See also: Part 4 - Studies by topic or subject**

→ **Note:** Country- or subject-specific studies on publishing and book development in East, West, Southern and Francophone Africa can be found under the appropriate headings in parts 3 and 4.

2313

Ellerman, Evelyn "The Literature Bureau: African influence in Papua New Guinea." *Research in African Literatures* 26, no. 4 (Winter 1995): 206-214.

A study of literature bureaux as agencies designed to serve the literary and educational needs of the newly literate. It traces the history and development of the East African Literature Bureau, which had served as a model for the establishment of the Papua New Guinea Literature Bureau, and compares the role, activities and success of the two organizations.

2314

Olden, Anthony *Libraries in Africa. Pioneers, policies, problems.* Lanham, MD: Scarecrow Press, 1995, 190 pp.

Chapter 6, (pp. 76-97) 'Reading Matter and Libraries for East Africans' contains an extensive discussion of the (now defunct) East African Literature Bureau under its director Charles Richards, and its role in the development of publishing and library services.

2315

Olden, Anthony "No Carpet on the Floor: extracts from the memoirs of Charles Granston Richards, Founding Director, East African Literature Bureau." *African Research and Documentation*, no. 71 (1996): 1-32.

> Extracts from the Richards papers (which are on deposit at the School of Oriental and African Studies, University of London), and which form an important historical record of the development of publishing, bookselling, and library services in East Africa. No Carpet on the Floor was written at the request of the University of Oxford Development Records Project, Rhodes House Library, and writing and revisions took place between 1977 and 1995. The extracts are a slightly abbreviated narrative of the years 1935 to 1965, and include accounts of Charles Richard's time with the CMS Bookshop in Nairobi (1935-1948); the East African Literature Bureau (1948-1963), and at OUP Eastern Africa (1963-1965). It also includes a section on the magazine *Tazama/Tunuulira* by David McD. Wilson, and an article on the establishment of public library services in East Africa by Sydney Hockey.

Africa, Francophone (General or regional studies on the francophone African book industries)

→   **See also: Part 4 - Studies by topic or subject**

2316

Akindes, Simon Adetona *The African Publisher: the cultural politics of indigenous publishing in Benin and Côte d'Ivoire.* [Unpublished; Ph.D. thesis, Ohio University, 1996.]

2317

Bugagbe, Agbessi "Il Faut Détruire le Livre qui Ramène en Arrière." *AfriquEducation* no. 13 (September 1995): 29-30.

> Interview with Christian Vandendriessche, cultural attaché at the French aid mission in the Central African Republic. Stresses the importance of school books, but also states that the educational book can be either the best or the worst of things. Condemns the bad practice of dumping out of date school books on Africa.

2318

Fofana, Souleymane "Il Faut Sortir de la Gratuit ." *AfriquEducation* no. 13 (September 1995): 28.

> An interview with Régine Fontaine, the official in charge of books at the Ministry of Cooperation in France, in which she defines French policy towards African educational books, and explains what action was taken after the devaluation of the CFA to avoid doubling of prices of school books.

2319

Haut Conseil de la Francophonie *La Production et la Diffusion des biens Culturels et Médiatiques de l'Afrique Francophone Sub-Saharienne.* Paris: Haut Conseil de la Francophonie (Les Cahiers de la Francophonie, 4), 1996. 182 pp.

Examines the production and distribution of cultural and multimedia materials (including books) in sub-Saharan francophone Africa, and the impact of new technologies on communication networks.

2320

Mateso, Emmanuel Locha (Transl. from the French by Diana Newton) "ACCT Support to Textbook Publishing in the South." *Bellagio Publishing Network Newsletter*, no. 17 (July 1996): 9-10.

An account of the work of ACCT's programme 'Edition scolaire du Sud' (Educational publishing in the South), and the agency's textbook support fund, notably in francophone Africa, which supports the production and distribution of educational tools, with a priority focus on textbooks for basic education.

2321

Mberio, Albert "Les Editeurs Etrangers n'ont Aucun Intérêt à Faire des Transferts de Technologie." *AfriquEducation* no. 13 (September 1995): 20, 22.

Address given by the Minister for Education of the Central African Republic to a seminar on educational book production and training. Underlines the lack of school texts and discusses the many obstacles to the production of good quality educational books in Africa.

2322

Mounkaila, Inazadan. "Editeurs 'Prète Nom': Mode d'Emploi." *AfriquEducation* no. 13 (September 1995): 35.

Discusses the practice of some publishing houses 'lending' their name to others and denounces this practice as being of no benefit to African publishers.

2323

Nnana-Rejasef, Marie-Claire "Livres Scolaires. Vers une guerre nord-sud?" *AfriquEducation* no. 13 (September 1995): 17-18.

Debates the necessity for Africa to produce its own educational books, and asks how this might be achieved. States that progress could be improved if the education sector was not seen as merely as a machine for spending money and suggests the integration of the education sector in a national book development strategy. Reiterates the need for cooperation and imaginative initiatives in the educational book production sector.

2324

Sylla, Ibrahima, and Fory Bah "Venance Kacou et Comlan Prosper Deh: nous voulons notre part du gâteau." *AfriquEducation* no. 13 (September 1995): 24, 26.
[Also published in *Le Livre Africain* no. 6, (September-October 1996): 11-13.]

Interview with the chief executives of Editions CEDA in Côte d'Ivoire and Editions CLE in Cameroun, during which both stress that policy makers and donors should work more close together to help the school book industry in Africa. Discusses the problems of funding, progress to date, and a plan of action for future development.

Africa, West (Regional studies)

→ **See also: Part 4 - Studies by topic or subject**

2325
Elaturoti, Folorunso "Data Generation and Utilization in Book Publishing within the West African Sub-Region." *The Publisher* 4, no. 1 (September 1996): 15-19.

> Examines the need for a data bank on all aspects of publishing, to aid the planning and successful execution of book production programmes, and to facilitate resource sharing among publishers in the West African sub-region. Sets out a proposed *modus operandi* for data gathering and for building up databases on pupil/student enrolment, infrastructural facilities for book production, sales outlets, authorship skills and resources, training and manpower development, shared mother-tongue languages, as well as bibliographic databases.

Africa, Southern (Regional studies)

→ **See also: Part 4 - Studies by topic or subject**

2326
Balkwill, Richard "The Publishing and Training Markets of Southern Africa. A review of current prospects. " *BDC Export News* September 1996: 10-11.

> Looks at new market opportunities in Southern Africa (primarily South Africa), for educational, academic and professional books, and the potential in the area of distance learning materials. Also briefly reviews the major retail outlets, and training for book industry personnel.

2327
Evans, Julie "The Southern African Book Scene: current issues for librarians, booksellers and publishers: some personal comments." *African Research and Documentation*, no. 71 (1996): 41-44.

> A summary of the papers presented at a seminar held during the 1996 London International Book Fair. (Note: papers are individually listed/abstracted elsewhere in the bibliography.)

2328
Reece, Jane "The Southern African Book Scene: current issues for librarians, booksellers and publishers." *Focus on International & Comparative Librarianship* 27, no. 2 (10 September 1996): 82-86.

> A further resumé of papers and discussions held at the 1996 LIBF seminar.

3   Country studies

→   **See also: Part 4 - Studies by topic or subject**

Benin

2329

de Souza, Oscar   "Publishing: A challenge in Benin." [Unpublished, photocopy; available from APNET, Harare, 1996, 3 pp.; also available in French "L'Edition: un défi au Bénin"]

> Paper presented to an APNET Seminar on Francophone and Anglophone Cooperation in Publishing, Accra, November 5-6, 1996. A short account of private sector publishing in Benin, and its present strengths and weaknesses.

2330

Médéhouégnon, Pierre, and Michel-Robert Gomez   "L'Edition et la Politique du Livre au Bénin: un défi à relever." *Notre Librairie* no. 124 (October/December 1995): 40-43.

> A short overview of the state of the publishing industry in Benin. Analyses the history of publishing since independence, and reviews the current state of production capacity and distribution outlets. Discusses the effect which the devaluation of the CFA had on the industry, and suggests co-publishing as a remedy to overcome chronic problems of funding and adequate distribution.

Côte d'Ivoire

2331

Palmeri, Robert J.   "Privatization of Publishing in the Côte d'Ivoire." In *The Challenge of the Market: privatization and publishing in Africa*, edited by Philip G. Altbach. Chestnut Hill, MA: Bellagio Publishing Network, Research and Information Center (Bellagio Studies in Publishing, 7), 1996, 79-93.

> Provides a historical background to publishing and the book market in French-speaking Africa in general, and the Côte d'Ivoire in particular. Examines the educational and trade publishing markets; the activities and shareholding, etc. of the two major publishing companies in the country, the Centre d'Edition et Distribution Africaine (CEDA) and Nouvelles Editions Ivoiriennes (NEI), their links with French publishing interests, and the emergence of several new independent presses. The dominance of one foreign publisher - Hachette, who now owns 40% of CEDA and 55% of NEI, together with Hachette's associated distribution company EDIPRESS which enjoys a virtual monopoly on newspaper and magazine publishing - is not seen as creating a favourable climate for the emergence of more private sector indigenous publishers, unless they are allowed to compete on an equitable basis and will get a fair share of the textbook markets, with adoption of some of their titles by the Ministry of Education. Also argues that meantime francophone African publishers must become more export-oriented, as they still export very little of their production even to adjacent francophone countries.

Eritrea

2332

Read, Tony *Eritrea. Educational Publishing Development and Textbook Provision. An analysis of the current situation with options for policy development* (1st draft). London: International Book Development Ltd., 1995. 20 pp. [restricted circulation?]

> Draft report on textbook provision for multiple language instruction in elementary schools in Eritrea, together with recommendations and strategies for the development of adequate local publishing capacity.

Ethiopia

2333

Wassie, Atnafu "Ethiopia: a new beginning in publishing." *Bellagio Publishing Network Newsletter*, no. 16 (Spring 1996): 9-11.

> An overview of the current situation of book publishing in Ethiopia. Examines the changing environment for publishing, problems faced by the book industries, and the challenges that lie ahead.

2334

Wassie, Atnafu "Privatization and the Challenges for Publishing in Ethiopia." In *The Challenge of the Market: privatization and publishing in Africa*, edited by Philip G. Altbach. Chestnut Hill, MA: Bellagio Publishing Network, Research and Information Center (Bellagio Studies in Publishing, 7), 1996, 47-61.

> The state's dominant role in the past in book development and publishing in Ethiopia has had a very negative effect, but the current government has now disengaged from its monopoly role in textbook publishing and has established clear policies on privatization. The author presents an overview of the publishing industry in the context of past developments and current problems, and examines factors such as the new language policy, the need for a national book policy, the challenges facing local writers, the deterioration of library services, and other pertinent issues. The author concludes that recent events have opened up a more favourable environment for book publishing, but that "its future is not dependent on privatization alone. The strategic involvement of the state and aid agencies is essential...to accelerate present activities toward the sustainable development of the publishing industry."

Ghana

2335

Bureau of Ghana Languages *The Bureau of Ghana Languages at a Glance*. Accra: Bureau of Ghana Languages, 1996. 26 pp.

> A short history of the Bureau of Ghana Languages and its role in publishing books in 11 Ghanaian languages. Includes some photographs of current and past members of staff.

2336

Crabbe, Richard A.B. "The Transition to Privatization in Publishing: Ghana's experience." In *The Challenge of the Market: privatization and publishing in Africa*, edited by Philip G. Altbach. Chestnut Hill, MA: Bellagio Publishing Network, Research and Information Center (Bellagio Studies in Publishing, 7), 1996, 29-46.

> Provides a historical background to state participation in publishing in Ghana, and describes how this had a highly detrimental effect on the development of the private sector book industry, who were largely excluded from the more profitable areas of educational publishing. This unfavourable climate has changed as from 1992 with more independent publishing companies emerging, though "full privatization has still a long way to go", and "the winds of change have been blowing slowly, and painfully so." The author examines how publishers have adapted to these changes, and looks at factors such as financing and profitability of publishing, the development of a national book policy, publishing capacity, training of book industry personnel, the role of book trade associations, distribution, library services in the country, publishing in Ghanaian languages, and the question of donor agency support. Concludes with a range of guidelines and "a checklist for privatizing the book industry", setting out the components which the author believes are essential integral parts in the growth of a thriving indigenous publishing industry.

2337

Dekutsey, Woeli "Are Ghanaian Publishers Producing Fewer Titles?" *Bellagio Publishing Network Newsletter*, no. 18 (November 1996): 10-11.

> Tries to find reasons for the declining publishing output from Ghanaian publishers, in particular that of Ghanaian publishers who are members of African Books Collective.

2338

Dekutsey, Woeli "Venture Capital in Ghana." [Unpublished, photocopy; available from CODE Europe, 1996, 3 pp.]

> Paper presented to a CODE Europe seminar on Commercial Development of African Publishing, Oxford, April 11-12, 1996. Examines the type of publishing businesses in Ghana and their capitalization structure.

2339

Ofei, Eric "The State of Publishing in Ghana Today." [Unpublished, photocopy; available from the author, c/o Afram Publications (Ghana) Ltd., PO Box M18, Accra]

> A synopsis of the current state of publishing in Ghana, reviewing national book policies, piracy, co-publishing, publishing capacity, financing of publishing ventures, and the role of the Ghana Book Publishers Association (GBPA).

Kenya

2340

Anon. "Company Profile: Focus Publications Ltd." *The East African Bookseller*, no. 13 (1996): 15-16.

> Short profile of Focus Publications Ltd., a Kenyan imprint launched in 1991, and their initial publishing programme.

2341

Chakava, Henry   "The Laws of Literacy." *Index on Censorship* 25, no. 2 (March/April 1996): 124-127.
[Also published, in slightly revised form and as "Publishing and State Censorship in Kenya", *Bellagio Publishing Network Newsletter*, no. 16 (Spring 1996): 12-14.]
> Examines manifestations of state censorship in Kenya, the banning of a number of publications, detention and harassment of writers, and systematic attempts to stifle creativity through curtailment of literary seminars, journals and writers' workshops, and a general lack of facilities or incentives to promote and reward academic excellence or creative talent. Also argues that the creation of state publishing institutions, which are largely controlling the textbook markets, represents another subtle form of censorship.

2342

Laurien, Ingrid "Emanzipation durch Geschichten-erzählen?" *Literatur Nachrichten*, no. 49 (April/June 1996): 12-14.
> Looks at the role of oral and grassroots literature in the emancipation of Kenyan women, and the activities of the Kenya Oral Literature Association and the Gender and Development Centre in Kisumu, headed by the Kenyan woman writer and publisher Asenath Bole Odaga.

2343

Munyiri, Wilfred   "100 Years of Printing and Publishing in Kenya." *The East African Bookseller*, no. 13 (1996): 10-14.
> An overview of the development of Kenya's publishing industry.

2344

< Muriithi, Felix   "Book Publishing Management: the challenge in Kenyan publishing." *Focus on International & Comparative Librarianship* 24, no. 1 (10 May 1993): 7-11.
On the needs and challenges of professional training for book industry personnel in Kenya.

2345

wa Kamau, Goro "High Cost of Books Making Reading Unaffordable." *The East African Bookseller*, no. 13 (1996): 24-25.
> Deplores the high cost of books in Kenya, and challenges publishers to explore alternative methods of book production and to learn from the experiences of other developing countries such as India.

2346

Waruingi, Gacheche   "Development of the Book Trade in Kenya." *African Publishing Review* 5, no. 3 (May/June 1996): 12.
> Excerpts from a speech given in November 1995 to the Kenya Booksellers' and Stationers' Association by the current Chair of the Kenya Publishers' Association, which looks at the bookseller-publisher relationship.

Malawi

2347

Chimombo, Steve *A Guide to Malawi's Literature.* Zomba, Malawi: Manchichi Publishing Company, 1996. 16 pp.

Includes a short section on Malawi's publishing industry, and a directory of publishers.

2348

Gurnah, Abdulrazak "A New Dawn in Malawi." *The Bookseller*, no. 4739, (18 October 1996): 26-27.

Following 30 years of repression under the regime of Hastings Kamusu Banda, Malawi's writers, intellectuals, and publishers, are looking forward to a new cultural environment. Here the distinguished Tanzanian writer Abdulrazak Gurnah reports on the poet's Frank Chipasula's vision of returning home from exile in the United States to organize the first Malawi literary festival and book exhibit.

Nigeria

2349

Adimorah, E.N.O. "Data Collection, Monitoring and Management: implications for book development." In *Creating a Conducive Environment for Book Publishing*, edited by Chukwuemeka Ike. Awka, Nigeria: Nigerian Book Foundation, 1996. 49-59.

The Director of Nigeria's National Information and Documentation Centre (NIDOC) argues that data collection plays a key part in book development. He sets out the opportunities offered by different databases, provides a short overview of data organization, data processing operations and database management, and assesses the likely benefits for Nigeria's book industries.

2350

Agbebi, E.A. "A Conceptual Framework for a Cost-Effective Book Distribution Network in Nigeria." In *Making Books Available and Affordable*, edited by Ezenwa-Ohaeto. Awka, Nigeria: Nigerian Book Foundation, 1995, 93-100.

Contends that existing book distribution systems are not responsive to the needs of Nigerian consumers. Examines a number of conventional book distribution systems and marketing channels, and proposes the establishment of a central distribution organization and book wholesale agency.

2351

Anon. "Nigeria's Economic Woes Threaten Book Industry." *NGAO. Newsletter of the Network for the Defence of Independent Media in Africa* 4, no. 30 (January 1996): 6.

Based on a Reuters report, draws attention to the Nigerian publishing industry "in a state of near collapse."

2352

Apeji, E. Adeche "Book Production in Nigeria: an historical survey." *Information Development* 12, no. 4 (December 1996): 210-214.

Reviews the historical background to the development of the Nigerian printing and book industries, and sees the early efforts of Christian missionaries as laying the foundation for "today's thriving [thriving?] book industries in Nigeria". Examines the government's involvement in publishing, the role of the multinationals, university press publishing, the activities of Franklin Book Programs in the 1960s, together with a brief note about indigenous initiatives.

2353

Apeji, E. Adeche "Developments in Education, Libraries and Book Publishing in Nigeria." *The Publisher* 4, no. 1 (September 1996): 19-24.

States that a flourishing book industry requires a harmonious relationship between the educational sector, libraries, and publishers. The contributions the multinational and other publishers have made in the provision of books in Nigeria depended to a large extent on developments in education and libraries. Conscious of these mutual relationships, the government should ensure, through deliberate policies, that "increase in enrolment is necessarily backed up by improved library and publishing facilities to meet new and increasing demand."

2354

Ezenwa-Ohaeto *Making Books Available and Affordable. Proceedings of the first annual national conference on book development, held at the National Theatre, Iganmu, Lagos, April 25-29, 1994.* Awka, Nigeria: Nigerian Book Foundation [PO Box 1132], 1995. 136 pp.

The papers (also individually abstracted) from a conference organized by the Nigerian Book Foundation, and which examined four possible solutions to overcome some of the formidable problems faced by the Nigerian book industries: (i) book subsidy schemes, (ii) self-sufficiency in materials for book production, (iii) exploitation of new technologies in book production, and (iv) establishing cost effective distribution and marketing networks. Also includes the recommendations which emerged from the conference and which will influence the programme of action of the Foundation in the years ahead.

2355

Fayose, Osazee "Data Collection: the foundation for effective book development." In *Creating a Conducive Environment for Book Publishing*, edited by Chukwuemeka Ike. Awka, Nigeria: Nigerian Book Foundation, 1996, 31-48.

The keynote address, by a Nigerian librarian, to the Nigerian Book Foundation's second national conference on book development, which focuses on the importance of data collection, the establishment of databases, the availability of data to aid the book industries, and the need to provide adequate bibliographic control.

2356

Ike, Chukwuemeka *Creating a Conducive Environment for Book Publishing. Proceedings of the Second Annual Conference on Book Development, 27 April 1995; and the Third National Conference on Book Development, 14 May 1996, held at the Conference Centre, University of Lagos, Nigeria.* Akwa, Nigeria: Nigerian Book Foundation [PO Box 1132], 1996. 249 pp.

Brings together the various presentations made at these two NBF conferences, as well as including the recommendations put forward at the meetings, and the text of the addresses presented during the formal opening ceremonies. The NBF's second conference concentrated on the need for data collection for the Nigerian book industries, while the third conference examined the ideal environment for nurturing authors, and author-publisher relations. The book also includes a study, by its Director, Chukwuemeka Ike, of the role of the NBF as a national book development organization with a review of its activities to date. (Note: most papers are individually listed/abstracted under various headings.)

2357

Jegede, Oluremi "Publications Laws of Nigeria: need for a review." *African Journal of Library, Archives & Information Science* 6, no. 1 (1996): 11-22.

Critically examines the various legal deposit laws currently in force in Nigeria. Discusses the probable reasons for non-compliance by publishers, and suggests new approaches, and new methods, that might be tried to enforce the law. It also calls for a draft model bill of publication law by the Law Reform Commission, which is necessary to encourage both Federal and state governments to review or enact publication laws, a bill that should reflect new advances in both educational, socio-cultural, and technological developments.

2358

Longe, H.O.D. "Developing a Database for Effective User Access in the Book Industry." In *Creating a Conducive Environment for Book Publishing*, edited by Chukwuemeka Ike. Awka, Nigeria: Nigerian Book Foundation, 1996, 58-65.

Argues that effective database systems are an essential requirement for the Nigerian book industries. Discusses the relevance of a distributed database approach in relation to data management, and analyses the different components required.

2359

Marinho, A.O. "Towards a Stable and Viable Environment for Primary Education in Nigeria." *The Publisher* 3, no. 2 (January 1996): 40-43.

Offers a number of ideas - including reading encouragement programmes - which, if implemented, are likely to facilitate the search for a stable and viable environment for the growth of primary education in Nigeria.

2360

< Mohammed, A. *The Role of Government in the Production, Supply and Distribution of Textbooks.* Lagos: Nigerian Educational Research & Development Council (NERDC), 1990. 67 pp.
[Conference proceedings/collection of papers; not examined.]

2361

Nwankwo, Victor "Working Capital in Nigerian Publishing." [Unpublished, photocopy; available from CODE Europe, Oxford, 6 pp.]

Paper presented to a CODE Europe seminar on Commercial Development of African Publishing, Oxford 11-12, 1996. Seeks to provide an overview of capital requirements for publishing in African countries, followed by a brief presentation of the financing of publishing in Nigeria.

2362

Olajide, Akin "The Book Problems of Primary Education in Nigeria." *The Publisher* 3, no. 2 (January 1996): 20-23.

Analyses the problems of book provision in support of primary education in Nigeria from two perspectives, (i) that of the consumer, and (ii) from the publisher's point of view. The author is critical of the government's attitude towards the publishing industry, and the ignorance on the part of government functionaries of understanding the nature of the book publishing business. Also puts forward a number of recommendations to promote the reading habit among Nigerian school children.

2363

Olaniowo, Wale "Nigeria: an overview of its publishing landscape." *The Publisher* 3, no. 2 (January 1996): 25-28.

Looks at the increasingly hostile business and economic environment in Nigeria, and as it is affecting the book industries. Questions why the publishing industry is in the doldrums despite operating in a country which claims to put massive resources into education, and attempts to provide some answers to these questions. Examines how Nigerian publishers are trying to survive in a country where educational institutions are now largely in disarray and where resources for books have become extremely scarce.

2364

Ogunleye, Bisi "Establishing a Cost-Effective National Book Distribution Network in Nigeria." In *Making Books Available and Affordable*, edited by Ezenwa-Ohaeto. Awka, Nigeria: Nigerian Book Foundation, 1995. 86-92.

Sets out a possible strategy for more effective distribution and marketing of Nigerian-published material, and proposes the establishment of a National Book Distribution Company, that would handle promotion and distribution both domestically and for markets elsewhere in Africa.

2365

Olude, O.O. "The National Book Distribution Network: suggestion for textbook distribution to schools." In *Making Books Available and Affordable*, edited by Ezenwa-Ohaeto. Awka, Nigeria: Nigerian Book Foundation, 1995, 101-107.

Reviews some of the current problems which affect book distribution of educational materials in Nigeria, and describes the rationale and working methods of the government-initiated Book Depot and Distribution Outlet (BDDO).

2366

< Okwilagwe, Andrew Oshiotse *Information Input as a Factor in Organizational Effectiveness of the Publishing Industry in Nigeria.* [Unpublished; Ph.D. thesis, University of Ibadan, 1993, 202 pp.]

2367

Saro-Wiwa, Ken "Notes of a Reluctant Publisher." *The African Book Publishing Record* 22, no. 4 (1996): 257-259.

> The late Ken Saro-Wiwa was an enterprising and innovative African publisher. On 10 November 1995, he was summarily and callously executed on the orders of the Nigerian junta despite pleas from world leaders to save his life. This article was submitted to ABPR as a provisional version in 1992, but he never managed to expand it as had been his wish. It was published posthumously by ABPR with only minor editorial changes, and as a tribute to Ken Saro-Wiwa. It provides an account of his school days as the scribe of school magazines, his first steps on "the painful path of self-publishing", and the setting up a "do-it-yourself operation" that became known as Saros International Publishers.

South Africa

2368

Anderson, Peter "Literary Publishing." In *How to Get Published in South Africa. A Guide for Authors* by Basil van Rooyen. Halfway House, South Africa: Southern Book Publishers, 2nd ed. 1996, 19-28.

> Provides guidance and tips how to get published in the field of literature, and surveys publishing outlets in South Africa in the four broad areas of literary writing: poetry, fiction, drama, and belles-lettres.

2369

Anon. "Easy-to-Read Books from ViVa." *African Publishing Review* 4, no. 6 (November/December 1995): 7.

> Profile of ViVa Books, an independent South African publishing house established in 1992, which specializes in publishing popular, culturally relevant, challenging, yet easy-to-read books for adults, school leavers, and those who have recently acquired reading skills.

2370

Coussy, Denise. "Hond Publishing, une Jeune Maison d'Edition." *Notre Librairie*, no. 123 (July-September 1995): 51-57.

> Interview with Timothy Duplessis and Rick Hatting, of Hond (and Taurus) Publishing in which they talk about publishing in a climate of censorship and repression during the apartheid days, and the challenges and risks of publishing in the 'new' South Africa for the small independent publisher.

2371

Ferguson, Gus "Thoughts on Publishing Poetry in South Africa." *Writers World*, no. 14 (1995): 14.

> A short profile, by its founder, of Snailpress - which "tries to put the poets first, offers royalties in advance, and does, within a non-budget, everything possible to distribute, sell and promote the books."

2372

Haricombe, Lorraine J., and Wilfrid F. Lancaster "Anatomy of a Book Boycott." *American Libraries* 26, (July/August 1995): 685-688.

> Describes the book boycott of South Africa during the Apartheid days, and measures taken by US libraries and institutions to prevent the importation and exportation of books and journals from/to South Africa.

2373

Horn, Caroline "South Africa's New Age." *The Bookseller*, no. 4730 (16 August 1996): 20-23.

> Meeting the educational needs of a South Africa in transition is creating huge headaches for publishers, not least among them the prospect of having to implement in three years the long-awaited new national curricula. However, as the author reports, the pain, and "the crisis management of the transition process", is mitigated by the excitement of participating in something new.

2374

Horwitz Gray, Eve "The Sad Ironies of South African Publishing Today." *Logos* 7, no. 4 (1996): 262-267.

> This is a sharp dissection of the current South African publishing scene. It paints a rather gloomy picture, and the author sums up the state of South African publishing today as being similar to the state of the nation: "There is panic and compliance; euphoria and despair; experimentation and stagnation; innovation and conservatism. The only certainty is transition. We can also report that transition is not a very comfortable state." The author deplores the fact that those South African publishers who were in the forefront of oppositional publishing during the apartheid years, are now the losers (or have been taken over by some large publishing conglomerate), and are not now enjoying a share of the more lucrative educational markets from which they were for so long politically excluded. The author states that the contents of textbooks now being published haven't thus far substantially changed, and self-serving systems in textbook supply which blighted the old regime remain. Publishing and the booktrade remains predominantly in white hands; creative literary lists - apart from the output of a few small presses - are still thin on the ground, and "the literary logjam will be broken only when the book industry more accurately represents the aspirations and needs of our diverse population."

2375

McCallum, Kate "State Publishing Looms in SA." *The Bookseller*, no. 4740 (27 October 1996): 10.

> Developments in educational circles in South Africa - and the announcement that a new syllabus implementation would be phased in at the start of the school year in January 1998 - have raised fears about the prospects of state publishing in South Africa. The author states that "there is a unanimity [among publishers, booksellers and others in the book industries] that state publishing would be an educational, political and economic disaster."

2376

Nassimbeni, Mary. "Collection Development in Public Libraries in South Africa: New library and language policies." *Library Acquisitions: Practice & Theory* 19, no. 3 (1995): 289-297.

> Seeks to explore the relationship between a new language policy in South Africa and collection development practice and policy, particularly in public libraries. Provides background to the national language debate and refers to publishing patterns and their effects on libraries' acquisitions practices. Implications for future acquisitions policy and practice are discussed in the light of the new language policy.

2377

Oliphant, Andries Walter "COSAW and Publishing for All." *Matatu*, no. 15/16 (1996): 173-182.

> COSAW Publishing was set up in 1987 as a semi-autonomous, income-generating operation owned by the Congress of South African Writers. This article provides some perspectives on the work of the organization and its publishing activities. It looks at the challenges in the years ahead for the small publishing house, including the publication of material in African languages, producing 'bare-foot' low cost publications aimed to provide outlets for beginners who participate in COSAW workshops in various regions, and the journal *Staffrider*. However, distribution networks are still dominated by the Anglo-American subsidiary Central News Agency (CNA), which has shown little interest in stocking and promoting the COSAW publishing output. The author concludes that "the growth of a viable indigenous publishing industry, capable of serving the needs of the majority of South Africans depends on the extent to which the broader social, economic and political changes break the monopolies and controls acquired by a racially inspired political economy in South Africa."

2378

Taylor, Sally "South Africa Today: an eye on the future." *Publishers Weekly*, (September 9, 1996): 43-59.

> A general overview of publishing and the book trade in South Africa today, with some coverage of book trade activities elsewhere in the region. Reports about the challenges faced by educational publishers, and also looks at academic and trade publishing, and the retail trade, including attempts to set up more book retailing outlets in the black communities.

2379

< van Gend, Cecily "The Independent Presses in South Africa." *Cape Librarian* 36, no. 7 (1992): 28-31.

Tanzania

2380

Lema, Elieshi "Venture Capital for Publishing in Tanzania: four cases." [Unpublished, photocopy; available from CODE Europe, 1996, 6 pp.]

> Paper presented to a CODE Europe seminar on Commercial Development of African Publishing, Oxford, April 11-12, 1996. Looks at venture capital for financing publishing

in Tanzania, and the difficulties encountered in raising capital or bank loans for publishing enterprises. Examines the case of one parastatal (Tanzania Publishing House), two private sector publishers (Ben & Company, and Mture Educational Publishers), and "Briefcase publishers".

Togo

2381

Ekue, Christiane Tchotcho   "Les Nouvelles Editions Africaines du Togo." [Unpublished, photocopy; available from APNET, 1996, 7 pp; also available in a French version, with identical title]

Paper presented to an APNET Seminar on Francophone and Anglophone Cooperation in Publishing, November 6-8, 1996. A profile of this major Togolese publisher, providing the background to its establishment, its corporate structure, the range of its publishing activities, its distribution methods, together with some views on possible South-South partnerships and co-publication programmes.

Uganda

2382

Ikoja-Odongo, J.R. "History of Books and Book Publishing in Uganda: 1876-1962." *Focus on International and Comparative Librarianship* 26, no. 2 (May 1995): 32-43.

A history of the book and publishing in Uganda up to the period of the country's independence. Provides a historical background, describes early publishing activities by Christian missionaries, educational and school book publishing by British multinational publishers, and publishing in African languages by the East African Literature Bureau. Also examines the role of local churches in the evolution of books in Uganda. Concludes with a look at book marketing and distribution at that time.

2383

Ikoja-Odongo, J.R. "The Book Industry in Uganda During the Post-Independence Period (1962-1988)." *Focus on International and Comparative Librarianship* 26, no. 2 (September 1995): 94-108.

The continuation of the preceding entry. An account "on that aspect of development in which Uganda has been a cripple, i.e. the book industry during the post-independence period." Reviews the founding of the state-supported Uganda Publishing House in a (short-lived) partnership with Macmillan's and the emergence of small independent publishers. Examines the reasons why some indigenous publishing initiatives failed. Also looks at the development of creative writing and readership, book distribution and the retail trade, and finds that indigenous publishers' promotion and book marketing leaves a great deal to be desired.

2384

Tumusiime, James "Uganda's Book Industry on the Way Back." *Uganda Book News* 1, no. 1 (January/March 1996): 4-7.
> The state of publishing and the book industries in Uganda is presently at the cross-roads. Here the Founder Chairman of the Uganda Publishers and Booksellers Association charts the industry's chequered past, and the growing opportunities that are now opening up for its recovery.

Zambia

2385

Munamwimbu, Ray "Privatization in Publishing: the Zambian experience." In *The Challenge of the Market: privatization and publishing in Africa*, edited by Philip G. Altbach. Chestnut Hill, MA: Bellagio Publishing Network, Research and Information Center (Bellagio Studies in Publishing, 7), 1996: 63-77.
> Provides a historical background to publishing in Zambia and reviews past state participation in publishing and international development assistance. Lack of competition from private sector companies contributed greatly to the decline of the book industry in the period up to 1991. However, a move by the government to embark on a policy of liberalization for the production and supply of educational materials as from 1992 has now created an enabling environment for the emergence of several new private sector publishing initiatives. Reviews aspects of competition, tendering and procurement systems, the market potential, the performance of private firms compared with parastatals, and the moves towards the establishment of a national book policy and a national book development council. Whereas privatization in publishing has now levelled the playing field, some problems remain however, particularly aspects of textbook development, bookselling, an equitable procurement system, together with other impediments such as lack of capital in an economy suffering from high inflation, and a lack of publishing expertise.

2386

Simwinga, Gideon "Publish or be Damned." *Orbit*, no. 60 (1st quarter 1996): 23-24.
> The publishing director of Multimedia Zambia argues that indigenous publishing is essential for a country's development, and examines Zambia's attempts to move away from   donated books to its own home-grown industry. The author also calls for positive government action to establish a comprehensive national book policy to map out a strategy and set the pace for the development of the book industry.

Zimbabwe

2387

Kumpmann, Ruth *Sprache, Literatur und Buchhandel in Zimbabwe.*
[Unpublished; Master's thesis, Institut für Völkerkunde und Afrikanistik, Ludwig-Maximilians-Universität, Munich, 1995, 155 pp.]

An MA thesis which examines the influence on publishing and the book trade amidst Zimbabwean writers' continuing and sometimes controversial debate on the choice of European or African languages as a medium of expression. Presents the current language situation in the country and the use of Shona, Ndebele and English; thereafter provides an overview of creative writing in these languages; followed by a detailed analysis of publishing output and the retail booktrade in Zimbabwe with profiles of individual publishers. The concluding section deals with the language debate, and as it affects the Zimbabwean book industries, setting out the different points of view and arguments by Zimbabwean writers, mostly through interviews.

4   Studies by topic or subject

Acquisition of African-published material

→   **See also: Libraries and publishing**

2388
<   Grover, Mark L. "Acquisition of Latin American Library Materials Published in Africa." *In Seminar on the Acquisition of Latin American Library Materials. Latin American Economic Issues: information needs and sources.* Los Angeles: SALALM Secretariat, Latin American Centre, University of California at Los Angeles, 1984, 293-301.

2389
Kagan, Alfred   "Sources for African Language Materials from the Countries of Anglophone Africa." *IFLA Journal* 22, no. 1 (1996): 42-45. [Originally listed as an unpublished IFLA conference paper, see main bibliography, item 1069]
[Also published in *Collection Building* 15, no. 2 (1996): 17-21]
> Provides guidance on how to acquire materials in African languages outside their countries of origin, and sets out the mechanisms in collecting this material. Notes the standard current reference sources, blanket and approval plan dealers, bookshops and publishers, printed and online catalogues, and two microform collections.

2390
McCartney, Murray   *APNET Open Forum: Library Acquisition of African Books, Harare, 2 August 1995.* Harare: African Publishers' Network, 1996 [Supplement to *African Publishing Review*, 5, no. 6, 1996]. 11 pp.
> Summary report of a meeting held during the 1995 Zimbabwe International Book Fair about the problems of acquisition of African books, and which looked at ways how the situation might be improved. Participants included both publishers and librarians.

2391
Pinfold, John "Acquiring Books from Southern Africa: a librarian's view." *Focus on International & Comparative Librarianship* 27, no. 2 (10 September 1996): 100-106.
[Also published in *African Research & Documentation*, no. 72 (1996): 54-59.]
> The Librarian at Rhodes House Library in Oxford (and current Chair of the Standing Conference on Library Materials on Africa/SCOLMA), provides a librarian's perspective how librarians find out what has been published in Southern Africa, how they go about acquiring such material, and what budgetary constraints they are working under and how they are coping with it. Reviews the various selection tools available and describes policies governing the acquisitions process.

2392

Raseroka, H.K. "Acquisition of African-published Materials by Libraries in Botswana - and Elsewhere in Africa." *Focus on International & Comparative Librararianship* 27, no. 2 (10 September) 1996: 86-87.
[Also published in *African Research & Documentation*, no. 72 (1996): 45-53]

The Librarian at the University of Botswana examines the problems facing acquisitions librarians in Africa in obtaining regular information of new African-published books, and the purchase of this material. Reviews collection development policies at the University of Botswana and then provides a detailed analysis of sources for selection of African-published material. The author is critical of African publishers' marketing strategies and the failure by some publishers to provide regular advance information and other promotional material, which are essential selection tools for librarians. The absence of effective distribution outlets, and bookselling methods which are not responsive to public needs, further aggravates the problem. The author also argues that "relationships among publishers, booksellers and librarians needs to be better understood by each group and be mutually supportive."

2393

Zell, Hans M. "African Serials Acquisitions by Libraries in the North - A survey." [Unpublished, photocopy; available from Hans Zell Publishing Consultants, Oxford [PO Box 56, Oxford OX1 2SJ] 1996, 8 pp.]
[Published in summary form only in *African Research & Documentation*, no. 72 (1996): 77-78]

The findings of a survey undertaken through a series of questionnaire mailings addressed to key Africana libraries in Europe, North America, and some elsewhere. The purpose of the survey was to shed light on the way in which libraries went about in selecting and purchasing their serials in general and those published in Africa in particular. Also surveys the increasing use of document delivery and inter-library loan for articles in African serials as a substitute for placing subscriptions.

African Books Collective Ltd. (ABC)

2394

Jay, Mary "The Book Chain: African Books Collective and UK book buyers." *Focus on International and Comparative Librarianship* 26, no. 2 (September 1995): 90-94.
[Also published in *African Research and Documentation*, no. 69 (1995): 30-33]

Outlines the services offered by the Oxford-based African Books Collective and the wide range of its promotional activities. Laments the current paucity of funding for book acquisitions for African studies and multicultural materials by UK public and academic libraries.

African languages, publishing in

2395

Chitsike, B.C. "Publishing in Indigenous Languages in Zimbabwe." *African Publishing Review* 5, no. 4 (July/August 1996): 5-6.

> An account of the development of publishing in Zimbabwe's two major national languages, Shona and Ndebele, and the pioneering role played by the Zimbabwe Literature Bureau (a government department in the Ministry of Education) in producing and distributing this material, and in encouraging authorship in these languages.

2396

Fajemisin, Martins Olusegun "An APNET Survey of Local Language Publishing: Part two: Kenya." *African Publishing Review* 4, no. 6 (November/December 1995): 5.

> A further extract from an important APNET-commissioned survey of African language publishing (see also main bibliography, items 1121 and 1222).

2397

Fajemisin, Martins Olusegun "An APNET Survey of Local Language Publishing: Part three: Togo."
African Publishing Review 5, no. 1 (March/April 1996): 5.

> Further extract (see entry 2396 above).

2398

Fajemisin, Martins Olusegun "An APNET Survey of Local Language Publishing: Part four: Zimbabwe." *African Publishing Review* 5, no. 2 (March/April 1996): 11.

> Further extract (see entry 2396 above).

2399

< Pugliese, Cristina *Author, Publisher and Gikuyu Nationalist. The life and writings of Gakaara wa Wanjau.* [Unpublished Ph.D. thesis, University of London, 1993]

2400

Reuster-Jahn, Uta. "The Entertainment Programme of Ndanda Mission Press: its contribution to Swahili literature in Tanzania." *Matatu*, no. 13/14 (1995): 339-352.

> Assesses the 'entertainment' programme of this Christian publishers' books in Kiswahili in promoting writing in African languages. Includes a bibliography of the Press's Kiswahili publications.

African Publishers' Network (APNET)

2401
Brickhill, Paul. "APNET: the African Publishers Network Report on Projects and Activities, 1st October 1993 to 30 September 1994." *Focus on International and Comparative Librarianship* 26, no. 2 (September 1995): 78-90.
[Also published in *African Research and Documentation*, no. 69 (1995): 34-46]
> Describes the principal objectives of the Harare-based African Publishers' Network, and provides a chronology of its varied activities between 1993 and 1994.

2402
Brickhill, Paul "News from the African Publisher's Network." *Bellagio Publishing Network Newsletter*, no. 16 (Spring 1996): 4-5.
> Looks back at APNET's activities and achievements as it celebrated its fourth anniversary on 17 February 1996.

2403
Echebiri, A.O. "Report on the Second General Council Meeting of the African Publishers' Network (APNET); Nairobi, Kenya, May 25-26, 1995" *The Publisher* 3, no. 2 (January 1996): 11-13.
> A report about the APNET 1995 Council meeting by the (then) President of the Nigerian Publishers Association.

Authors and publishers/The role of the writer

→   **See also: Copyright**
   Publishing, of African writers and African literature

2404
Awolalu, Tosin "Beyond Patronage and the Spilt Ink." In *Creating a Conducive Environment for Book Publishing*, edited by Chukwuemeka Ike. Awka, Nigeria: Nigerian Book Foundation, 1996, 184-207.
> Asks whether the current environment in Nigeria can support primary authorship. The author finds that "the environment that produced the first generation of Nigerian authors had greater consideration for literary merit than other factors in arriving at publishing decisions", that "there is a great literary inertia in Nigeria" at the present time, and that it has become very difficult for the new generation of Nigerian authors to get publishers to accept manuscripts of creative writing. The author is sympathetic with the enormous problems faced by the Nigerian book industries, but also critical of Nigerian publisher's lack of encouragement and active support of authorship, and of those publishers "who do not rank high in integrity when it comes to matters of royalties or other earnings due to authors." He also reports about a study undertaken by the Association of Nigerian authors which sought to determine the extent of author satisfaction with their publishers. The author concludes by calling on publishers "to wake up and initiate an aggressive bookshop development programme because in it lies the future of the traditional publisher's market."

2405

Ekwensi, Cyprian D. "Creative a Conducive Environment for Authorship." In *Creating a Conducive Environment for Book Publishing*, edited by Chukwuemeka Ike. Awka, Nigeria: Nigerian Book Foundation, 1996, 160-173.

A contribution to the debate on a conducive environment for authorship by the distinguished Nigerian writer Cyprian Ekwensi, who states that "Nigeria has a world bank of ideas and remedies until it comes to implementation" and that an awareness of professional authorship doesn't exist, much less an enabling atmosphere. He is also critical of cavalier attitudes to copyright and the rights of authors in Nigeria, both by individuals and by the government; and examines author-publisher relations and urges publishers to become more export-oriented. Concludes that "a conducive atmosphere is a product of several factors working together or at times independently" and that "above all else, political stability remains the most conducive atmosphere of all."

2406

Ike, Chukwuemeka "Creating a Conducive Environment for Authorship." In *Creating a Conducive Environment for Book Publishing*, edited by Chukwuemeka Ike. Awka, Nigeria: Nigerian Book Foundation, 1996, 78-137.

The President of the Nigerian Book Foundation, and also a prolific and widely published Nigerian writer, sets out his concept of authorship and puts forward a wide range of recommendations covering areas in which positive action is required by the Nigerian government to help create a conducive environment for authorship in the country. He then examines the role of the formal education sector, the role of family and society, the role of publishers and bookseller, that of libraries and information services, as well as the role of authors and writers' associations. He also critically examines author-publisher relations, and argues that Nigerian publishers must become more aggressive in their marketing methods both at home and overseas and, in particular, calls for more optimum exploitation of subsidiary rights, i.e. digest and book condensation rights, first serialization rights, translation rights, or dramatic, film, TV and broadcasting rights, etc. Nigerian publishers "have the tendency to pad their publishing agreements with these subsidiary rights even though they know they have no intention of, or capacity, for exploiting them."

2407

Korley, Nii Laryea "Ayi Kwei Armah Speaks." *West Africa*, no. 4128 (9-15 December 1996): 1923-1924

An interview with the distinguished Ghanaian writer Ayi Kwei Armah, now resident in Senegal, and who has recently established his own publishing company called Per Ankh, which means The House of Life in ancient Egyptian.

2408

Lawal-Solarin, O.M. "Creating a Conducive Environment for Authorship: contribution by a publisher." In *Creating a Conducive Environment for Book Publishing*, edited by Chukwuemeka Ike. Awka, Nigeria: Nigerian Book Foundation, 1996, 174-183.

[Also published in *The Publisher* 4, no. 1 (September 1996): 6-8.]

A publisher's perspective on the debate, and a response to Ike (see 2406), by the current President of the Nigerian Publishers' Association. Examines the concept of authorship and what constitutes 'a conducive environment', and cautions against a tendency to compare the Nigerian situation with that prevailing in countries in the North, where disposable income is much higher. Also looks at the role of government and at author-publisher relations and says "publisher must now protest cruelty to Nigerian publishers by authors who have nothing good to say about publishers." Reports about the Nigerian Publishers' Association Code of Conduct and refutes the charges of non-payment of royalties. Argues that the economic crisis in the country has had a detrimental effect on every aspect of the book industry: authorship, publishing, printing and distribution, and that it is up to the government to create an enabling environment for the book industries.

2409

Ripken, Peter "Creating a Conducive Environment for Authorship." In *Creating a Conducive Environment for Book Publishing*, edited by Chukwuemeka Ike. Awka, Nigeria: Nigerian Book Foundation, 1996, 138-145.

> A keynote address delivered to a Nigerian Book Foundation conference in 1996 by the director of the Frankfurt-based Society for the Promotion of African, Asian and Latin American Literatures. Regrets the fact that much of the debate about African writing takes place outside Africa, and "does not reach those in Africa who want to write, and want to write better than those who have written before them."

2410

Umomadu, N.O. "A Response to Creating a Conducive Environment for Authorship." In *Creating a Conducive Environment for Book Publishing*, edited by Chukwuemeka Ike. Awka, Nigeria: Nigerian Book Foundation, 1996, 146-159

> A response to Ike (see entry 2406 above) sounding a few caveats, especially about calls for action on the part of the government, which "given our well known Nigerian attitude... will sound like the indistinguishable cacophony of animal and reptilian voices on a starless night." The author is scathing about ostentatious book launches in Nigeria, and equally critical about Nigerian publishers. He claims "the books Nigerian publishers publish never get promoted", royalties are not "correct", and royalty advances non-existent; the retail booktrade is in a sorry state, book prices have sky-rocketed and piracy is rife. Public libraries are unable to assume an active role in book development because they are grossly underfunded and their shelves are mostly empty.

Bellagio Publishing Network

→ See also: Book and journals assistance and donation programmes

2411

Salahi, Katherine. "Bellagio Donors, APNET Meet in Oxford." *Bellagio Publishing Network Newsletter*, no. 15 (November 1995): 2-3.

> A report about a meeting of donors from the Bellagio Publishing Network and representatives of the African Publishers' Network, discussing APNET's future range of activities and funding needs.

Book and journals assistance and donation programmes/ Book subsidy schemes

→ **See also: Bellagio Publishing Network**

2412

Balarabe, Ahmed Abdu. "Nigerian University Libraries and the World Bank Loan." *Third World Libraries* 5, no. 2 (Spring 1995): 31-45.

A critical examination of the World Bank Federal Universities Adjustment Loan Project, for the provision of books and journals, information technology facilities and equipment, and staff development in Nigerian libraries. Reviews how the project has benefited Nigerian university libraries, but also reports about problems of journals supply and book procurement, caused by lack of current selection tools and inaccessibility to major international bibliographic databases, and problems with, and disagreements among, suppliers.

2413

Book Aid International *Annual Review 1995*. London: Book Aid International, 1996. 12 pp.

Annual report of the major UK book charity Book Aid International which sends eighty per cent of its books to countries in sub-Saharan Africa, where there is a huge and growing need. BAI also supports indigenous African publishing through various schemes, including the Intra-African Book Support Scheme, operated in collaboration with African Books Collective Ltd.

2414

Doust, Robin W. "Books for Zimbabwe." *The Zimbabwean Review* 2, no. 2 (April-June 1996): 11-12.

The Chief Librarian at Bulawayo City Library assesses a Book Aid International consultancy report (by John Salter) about book supply and book donation schemes in/for Zimbabwe.

2415

Ekpo, Moses F. "The Berne Convention: implications for book subsidy schemes and availability of books." In *Making Books Available and Affordable*, edited by Ezenwa-Ohaeto. Awka, Nigeria: Nigerian Book Foundation, 1995, 18-24.

Examines the implications of a number of programmes and subsidy schemes established by the Nigerian government with regard to copyright conventions, the special provisions for developing countries and the aspect of compulsory licensing. Reviews the work of the Nigerian Copyright Council as it assists publishers to tackle problems of book scarcity in the country.

2416

Friends-of-the Book Foundation *Friends-of-the Book Foundation*. Nairobi: Friends-of-the Book Foundation [PO Box 39624], n.d. [1996?]. 25 pp.

A profile of the Nairobi-based Friends-of-the-Book Foundation, a non-profit organization established to help alleviate the book famine in East Africa and to promote functional literacy. The organization facilitates the publication/translation (both in Kiswahili and in English) of key books for the reading public, and at affordable prices. The booklet sets out the background to the establishment of the organization, its principal objectives, details of books published to date and those in the pipeline.

2417

Momoh, Ansu E. "Programs Discussed at Nairobi World Bank Book Seminar." *Bellagio Publishing Network Newsletter*, no. 15 (November 1995): 6-7.

Reports about a roundtable discussion held between leading indigenous African publishers and senior World Bank officials in Nairobi in May 1995, one of whose principal objectives was to educate African publishers on the operations of the World Bank regarding competitive bidding, and the Bank's procurement policies.

2418

Newton, Diana. "A New Canadian Program: The International Publishing Partnership." *Bellagio Publishing Network Newsletter*, no. 15 (November 1995): 13-14.

Reports about a new not-for-profit initiative, the International Publishing Partnership (IPP), funded by the Canadian International Development Agency (CIDA) and the Canadian publishing industry, which "seeks to offer an alternative to the status quo of past projects designed by non-publishers, often unfamiliar with the nature and fundamental principles of publishing."

2419

Orimalade, Oluronke "Book Subsidy Schemes: an international perspective." In *Making Books Available and Affordable*, edited by Ezenwa-Ohaeto. Awka, Nigeria: Nigerian Book Foundation, 1995, 8-17.

[previously published in *African Publishing Review* 3, no. 6 (November/December 1994): 1-2; and in *The Publisher* 3, no. 1 (January 1995): 22-23; see main bibliography, entry 1226]

Examines the nature of book subsidy schemes in Europe, North America, Australia, India, and in Africa.

2420

Priestley, Carol, and Graham Rowbotham, comps. *INASP [International Network for the Availability of Scientific Publications] Directory 1996.* London: INASP [PO Box 2564, London W5 1ZD] and ICSU Press, 1996. 207 pp.

A new and updated edition of this reference tool (for previous editions see main bibliography items 1234 and 1241). Provides full information on some 200 organizations, institutions, learned societies, professional associations, and foundations involved in book and journal donation schemes, including both subject-specific organizations in particular areas of the sciences, or organizations who include library and book development as one of their areas of interest

2421

Rosenberg, Diana "The African Journals Distribution Programme: an evaluation of the pilot project." *African Publishing Review* 5, no. 1 (January/February) 1996: 6-7.

[Slightly shorter version, "The African Journals Distribution Program: an update", also published in *Bellagio Publishing Network Newsletter*, no. 15, (November 1995): 8-9]

> Reports about an evaluation exercise of the first year of the African Journals Distribution Program (AJDP), a project which aims to strengthen the African academic journal publishing sector.

2422

Rosenberg, Diana   "African Journals Distribution Programme." *Focus on International & Comparative Librarianship* 27, no. 2 (10 September 1996): 115-120.

> Sets out the needs, objectives and *modus operandi* of the African Journals Distribution Programme (AJDP), a scheme through which scholarly journals published in African countries are made available to scholars and academics in other African countries. To do this the Programme purchases subscriptions on behalf of university libraries in Africa. Also includes an evaluation of the pilot year (1994), when 18 scholarly journals published in 9 African countries were purchased and distributed in 8 anglophone African countries.

2423

Sharples, Carolyn "Journals for African Universities." *Focus on International & Comparative Librarianship* 25, no. 3 (31 December 1994): 133-137.

> Reports about the work of International Campus Book Link (ICBL), which aims to help fill a small part of the need for tertiary materials by supplying academic journals and books to its partners and recipient libraries in Sub-Saharan Africa.

2424

Taylor, Ian "World Bank in Turmoil." *The Bookseller* (7 June 1996): 11.

> The author, the (UK) Publishers Association's international director, says the World Bank is at present in turmoil as the Bank undergoes reorganization, and the big tertiary book procurement projects of the late 1980s are a thing of the past.

2425

Thomas, Akin "A Book Subsidy Scheme for Nigeria: the way forward." In *Making Books Available and Affordable*, edited by Ezenwa-Ohaeto. Awka, Nigeria: Nigerian Book Foundation, 1995, 25-38.

> Provides some historical background to educational publishing in Nigeria and assesses the potential market for books on the basis of enrolment of school pupils and students at institutions of higher learning. The author is critical of the lack of government support for the educational book industry, and states that despite pious pronouncements by various government officials over the past two decades little progress has been made, and the government is still to implement most of the recommendations and resolutions passed at numerous conferences. Defines his own concept of 'subsidy', which he sees in a broader sense of support for authorship, book design and illustrations, editing, printing and binding, marketing and distribution, libraries, as well as other areas of support such as fellowship awards, sponsorship of literary awards, or (citing the Norwegian model) support by way of purchase of bulk quantities of books from Nigerian publishers for distribution to libraries throughout the country.

2426

Ziegler, Philip "Book Aid International." *The Author* Autumn (1996): 107.

> A short profile of Book Aid International (formerly Ranfurly Library Services), how it has developed over the years, and its principal activities.

Book development councils (and other book promotional organizations)

→ See also: Book trade associations

2427

Dektusey, Woeli "Meet Mr. Book Development." *Ghana Book News* 2, no. 1 (April 1996): 3-4.

> A profile of Amu Djoleto the founder and former Director of the Ghana Book Development Council (GBDC), and its activities in support of Ghana's book industries.

2428

Makhubela, L.   "The Book Development Council of South Africa: making a difference in building an information literate South Africa." *Innovation* [Pietermaritzburg] 10, (June 1995): 41-44.

> An account of the establishment of the Book Development Council of South Africa (BDCSA) reviewing its plans and activities to date, and the challenges it faces in achieving its aims and objectives. Argues for the need of a national book policy and calls for the setting up of provincial branches of the BDSCA.

Book fairs (General)

→ See also: Zimbabwe International Book Fair

2429

Bugembe, Mary "Pan-African Children's Book Fair Grows in Importance." *Bellagio Publishing Network Newsletter*, no. 18 (November 1996): 7-8.

> The Director of the Pan-African Children's Book Fair, held annually in Nairobi, reviews the achievements of the Fair to date, and the challenges that lie ahead.

2430

Foire Internationale du Livre et du Matériel Didactique *5ème Foire International du Livre et du Matériel Didactique, du 5 Décembre au 11 Décembre 1995. Catalogue Officielle.* Dakar: Foire International du Livre et du Matérial Didactique, 1995. 52 pp.

> The official fair catalogue and programme of the 5th Dakar International Book Fair, including full names and addresses (and telephone/fax numbers for most) of exhibitors, and exhibitors classified by subject interests and areas of specialization.

2431

Ghana International Book Fair *1st Ghana International Book Fair. Catalogue.* Accra: Ghana International Book Fair/Ghana Trade Fair Authority, 1996. 30 pp. (with loose insert, Souvenir Programme, 8 pp.)
> The official fair catalogue and programme of the 1st Ghana International Book Fair, including full names and addresses (and telephone/fax numbers for most) of all exhibitors.

2432

Gibbs, James "Of Filthy Lucre and Words." *West Africa*, no. 4118 (23-29 September 1996): 1529.
> A preview of the 1st Ghana International Book Fair, looking back at some earlier book fairs held in Ghana, and examining author-publisher-bookseller relations.

2433

Higo, Aigboje "The Usefulness of Book Fairs to African Publishers." [Unpublished, photocopy; available from Bellagio Publishing Network Secretariat, Oxford, 1996, 6 pp.]
> Paper presented at the Bellagio Publishing Network Round Table on Book Fairs, Accra, November 8, 1996. Reviews the principal book fairs in Africa and their contribution to book promotion on the continent.

2434

Martin, David "The Future of African Book Fairs." [Unpublished, photocopy; available from the Bellagio Publishing Network Secretariat, Oxford, 7 pp.]
> Paper delivered at the Bellagio Publishing Network Round Table on Book Fairs, Accra, November 8, 1996. The founder (and Director for the first four years) of the Zimbabwe International Book Fair charts the growth of book fairs in Africa and the ZIBF in particular. Expresses some qualms regarding the future direction of ZIBF, and voices some of his concerns regarding the proliferation of African book fairs in general. Suggests the setting up of a Pan-African book fair organization, to act as a guiding body to mobilize support for book fairs on the continent, and to stage a continental Pan-African book fair, which should be interspersed with the holding of regional book fairs in various parts of Africa.

2435

Mugo, Macharia (ed.) *5th Pan African Children's Book Fair Magazine* (May 27th-31st, 1996). Nairobi: CHISCI Press, 1996. 44 pp.
> The official exhibitor catalogue and companion to the 5th Pan-African Children's Book Fair. In addition to the full programme and exhibitor listings, etc., the magazine contains a number of short contributions on writing and publishing for children and the 'Children's Reading Tent', which is now a well-established feature at the Fair. Enclosed as a loose insert: "The Pan African Children's Bookfair. From Experimentation to Institutionalisation" by Mary Bugembe, which gives the background to the Fair, how it is organized, and describes activities during the Fair; also provides some statistical analysis of exhibitor and visitor participation since the first Fair was held in 1992.

2436

Mundondo, Tainie "Pan-African Children's Book Fair (PACBF)." *African Publishing Review* 5, no. 5 (September-October 1996): 9.

> The Pan-African Children's Book Fair is one of several book fairs supported by the African Publishers' Network (APNET), and in 1996 APNET sponsored nine African publishers to attend. It also arranged for a collective exhibit displaying 225 titles from 54 publishers in 16 countries. Reports about the opportunities offered by the Fair, and the benefits to APNET members.

2437

Ogolla, James "The Utility of the Pan-African Children's Book Fair to African Publishers." In *5th Pan African Children's Book Fair Magazine.* Nairobi: CHISCI Press, 1996, 11-13.

> The Publicity Manager of a Kenyan publishing company appraises the achievements of the Pan-African Children's Book Fair and finds that publishers have both learned a great deal from it through their participation, as well as having benefited from it in terms of sales. He calls on Kenyan publishers to "wean, nourish, nurture and develop it" to the benefit of all those in the book industries.

2438

Paradza, Vonai "Frankfurt Book Fair, 11 to 16 October 1995" *African Publishing Review* 5, no. 1 (January/February 1996): 12.

> A member of staff of Mambo Press, Zimbabwe, reports about her attendance at the 1995 Frankfurt Book Fair on behalf of the Zimbabwe Book Publishers Association.

2439

Randle, Ian "South-South Co-operation: do book fairs help?" [Unpublished, photocopy; available from the Bellagio Publishing Network Secretariat, Oxford, 1996, 3 pp.]

> Discussion paper presented to the Bellagio Publishing Network Round Table on Book Fairs, Accra, November 8, 1996. Presents the perspective of a publisher from the Caribbean on the opportunities that are available at book fairs to foster cooperation on a South-South basis. The author also critically assesses the values and likely benefits of book fair participation, and reviews his own participation - with a collective Caribbean exhibit - at three successive Zimbabwe International Book Fairs.

Book prizes and awards (General)

→ **See also: Noma Award for Publishing in Africa**

2440

Anon. "Commonwealth Writers' Prize." *African Publishing Review* 4, no. 6 (November/December 1995): 8-9.

> A report about the 1995 Commonwealth Writers' Prize, and the winners in the categories of 'Best Book - Africa Region' and 'Best First Book - Africa Region'.

Book promotion and marketing (including export promotion)

→ **See also: African Books Collective Ltd.**
Book Fairs (General)
Zimbabwe International Book Fair

2441

Bamhare, Miriam "Zimbabwe Celebrates its Second Annual National Book Week."
African Publishing Review 5, no. 4 (July/August) 1996: 10-11.

> The Executive Director of the Zimbabwe Book Development Council reports about a successful book promotional event held in Zimbabwe in 1995, which included public readings and poetry recitals, competitions, and an interactive theatre production on the problems of reading promotion in schools.

2442

Chakava, Henry "Book Marketing and Distribution: the Achilles' Heel of African Publishing." In *Publishing in Africa: one man's perspective*, by Henry Chakava. Chestnut Hill, MA: Bellagio Publishing Network, Research and Information Center (Bellagio Studies in Publishing, 6), 1996, 109-133.

> Looks at the challenges of book distribution in Africa today. Presents an overview of book promotion and marketing strategies available to the African book industry, and examines "the extent to which these marketing possibilities are being exploited by the African publisher today." Finds that marketing and promotion by many African publishers is frequently feeble; there is lack of advance information about new books, unattractive and ineffective promotion material, and some African publisher's failure to make use of the many opportunities that exist for free publicity and listings of their books in the major bibliographic services. The author is also critical of the sometimes sub-standard production quality of African-published books, sloppy editing and proofreading, poor binding and finishing; or books which lack proper title pages and essential copyright data, have no ISBNs, and which show evidence of "lack of proper quality controls and discipline at all levels of the African book publishing chain." Also considers the role of book development councils and national publishers associations, and makes a number of recommendations how to tackle the problems of book marketing and distribution in Africa. Concludes that although marketing and distribution comes at the end of the publishing process it will determine "success or failure of any publishing house".

Bookselling and book distribution

→   See also: **African Books Collective Ltd.**
         Intra-African book trade

2443
Mosura, Kolade   "Information Generation and Utilisation in Bookshops and Libraries." In *Creating a Conducive Environment for Book Publishing*, edited by Chukwuemeka Ike. Awka, Nigeria: Nigerian Book Foundation, 1996, 66-70.

> Makes some suggestions for good practice in bookselling, reviews some tools of the trade, and stresses the need for proper management information systems and adequate stock control.

2444
Orimalade, Oluronke   "Retailing Books on Women in Nigeria Requires More Than Just Selling Books." [Unpublished, photocopy; available from the author, c/o University of Lagos Bookshop, 1996, 9 pp.]

> Paper given at the Southern Partners Project Workshop, Zimbabwe International Book Fair, August 2, 1996. Assesses the advancement of women in the Nigerian business sector, and their aptitude for entering the book trade. Also examines publishing of books on women in Nigeria, how they are sold and retailed in the country, and makes some suggestions for more effective distribution channels.

Book trade associations

→   See also: **African Books Collective Ltd.**
         African Publishers' Network
         Book development councils

2445
Nigerian Publishers' Association   *Code of Conduct. Memorandum & Articles of Association*. Ibadan: Nigerian Publishers Association, 1996. 28 pp.

> Includes the Nigerian Publishers' Association Memorandum of Association, as well as a self-imposed Code of Conduct, which aims to make it clear that NPA are committed to the maintenance of high ethical and professional standards.

Children's book publishing

2446
Boye, Mary   "Practices and Variables Affecting the Quality of Ghanaian's Children's Literature." *African Journal of Library, Archives & Information Science* 3, no. 1 (April 1993): 35-44.

2447

Bugembe, Mary   "African Publishers Form Consortium to Promote the Development, Publishing and Marketing of Children's Science Books." [Unpublished, photocopy; available from Bellagio Publishing Network Secretariat, Oxford, 1996, 12 pp.]

> Paper presented at the Bellagio Publishing Network Meeting, Addis Ababa, November 21-22, 1996. Describes a new initiative whereby eight African publishers have formed themselves into a consortium - in partnership with the British publisher Belitha Press - to publish co-editions of children's science publications originally published in the North.

2448

Fayose, P.O. *A Guide to Children's Literature for African Teachers, Librarians and Parents*. Ibadan: AENL Educational Publishers, 1995. 132 pp.

> A bibliography of 628 annotated entries (in English and some in French), arranged by type of materials, i. e. picture-story books, fairy tales, poetry, drama, etc.. With country and author indexes.

2449

Fayose, P.O. *Nigerian Children's Literature in English*. Ibadan: AENL Educational Publishers, 1995. 116 pp.

> Critical review of Nigerian children's books, arranged by type of books. Also includes biographical profiles of some of the best known Nigerian children's writers.

2450

Heale, Jay "Which Way the Wind Blows?" *Writers World*, no. 13 (1994): 33-34.

> Looks at trends in children's book publishing in South Africa, and states that it is not so much a matter of teaching children how to read, but that there will have to be teaching that will make children want to read, and that reading should be fun.

2451

Kamani, Wacango   "Gender Analysis in Book Publishing." In *5th Pan African Children's Book Fair Magazine*. Nairobi: CHISCI Press, 1996, 19-21.

> Draws attention to the need of children's books to come under scrutiny and that they must be gender sensitive, gender responsive and gender balanced. For example, in many traditional stories girls are always portrayed as victims - "caught by the ogre only to cry feebly for help" - whereas boys never have such problems! Reports how a number of Kenyan publishers are dealing with this situation and have deliberately incorporated gender screening in their publishing policy. The author argues that "gender sensitisation and training is necessary for publishers to understand the social order that sets our society's thinking."

2452

Lema, Elieshi   "The Children's Book Project for Tanzania." [Unpublished, photocopy; available from CODE Europe, 1996, 14 pp.]

> Paper presented to the CODE Europe seminar on The Commercial Development of African Publishing, Oxford, April 11-12, 1996. Provides the background that led to the establishment of the CODE-initiated Children's Book Project for Tanzania, its structure,

how it works, its achievements to date, problems and lessons learned, and possible future directions.

2453

Okoye, Ifeoma   "Auf der Suche nach Lesern für Kinderbücher." *Literatur Nachrichten*, no. 51 (October-December 1996): 15-16.

> A prominent Nigerian children's writer looks at the current state of publishing for children in Nigeria and finds that the picture is not a happy one. Most Nigerian publishers concentrate in producing school and educational texts, and neglect literature for enjoyment reading rather than for passing examinations; children's books are rarely reviewed in the press. And while folktales have some value, children in Nigeria today want books that reflect contemporary interests and realities, and topics with which they can identify.

2454

Okoye, Ifeoma "In Search of a Child Reader and a Writer of Children's Books." In *Creating a Conducive Environment for Book Publishing*, edited by Chukwuemeka Ike. Awka, Nigeria: Nigerian Book Foundation, 1996, 208-217

> A fuller (English) version of the preceding entry. Laments the fact that "publishing for children is in a very poor state in Nigeria today", with writing for the very young children in their most formative years being the most seriously neglected. Makes a number of suggestions for more effective promotion of the reading habit.

2455

< Omowunmi, Segun "Children's Magazines in Africa." *Bookbird* 28, (May 1990): 4-5.

> A brief survey of a number of African-published children's magazines.

2456

Potgieter, Alida "Children's Book Publishing in South Africa." In *How to Get Published in South Africa*, by Basil van Rooyen. Halfway House, South Africa: Southern Book Publishers, 2nd ed. 1996, 29-37

> Looks at the opportunities that exist in South for publication of children's books for the general market. Examines market constraints, language issues, children's book awards, and the type of fiction and non-fiction books published by South African imprints, and how these publishers evaluate manuscript proposals and come to a publishing decision.

2457

< Randall, Isobel "Publishing Children's Books in South Africa: a courageous venture in an apartheid society." *Bookbird* 27, (September 1989): 5-6.

> Largely on the publishing activities - in the area of children's books - of Ravan Press.

Community and rural publishing

2458

Ngeze, Pius B. (ed.) *Seminar on Techniques for Writing, Editing, Publishing and Distributing Reading Materials in Rural Areas.* Bukoba, Tanzania: Kagera Writers and Publishers Co-operative Society [PO Box 1222], 1991, 84 pp.
> The proceedings of a UNESCO co-sponsored seminar held in Tanzania in 1989 on writing, publishing, and distributing materials for rural communities. Contains contributions in English and in Kiswahili.

Copyright

→ **See also: Rights sales, licensing and co-publishing**

2459

Aganahi, Rock-Maxime "La Piraterie des Oeuvres Littéraires et Artistiques est un Fléau Planétaire qui cause des Dommages Importants." *Le Livre Africaine*, no. 5, (1996): 15-16.
> Interview with Samuel Ahokpa, director of the Bureau Béninoise des Droits d'Auteur (BUBEDRA), in which the latter reports about a fact-finding investigation undertaken by BUBEDRA on copyright issues, and infringements, in Benin, and measures taken to protect the rights of authors.

2460

Bonde, D. "Copyright and the Right to Write." *Moto*, no. 124 (1993): 8-10, 17.
> On copyright issues affecting African writers.

2461

< Kukubo, Robert J. "Copyright Laws of Botswana, Lesotho and Swaziland: an historical overview." *Mohlomi*, no. 6 (1990): 1-53.

2462

Momoh, Ansu "'Thou Shalt Not Steal': another look at copyright." *African Publishing Review* 5, no. 1 (January/February) 1996: 14-15.
> Examines the fundamental principles or concepts which copyright legislation in any country must maintain, and describes the main international copyright conventions and their special provisions for developing countries.

2463

Rudolph, John-Willy "Why are Intellectual Property Rights Important? What Mechanisms Constrain or Encourage Creation and Proper Utilization of Intellectual Property?" In *National Book Policies for Africa*, edited by Murray McCartney. Harare: Zimbabwe International Book Fair Trust, 1996, 42-46.
> The Executive Director of Kopinor, the Norwegian Reproduction Rights Organization, states the case for the establishment of more collective Reproduction Rights

Organizations in Africa (they currently exist in South Africa, Kenya and Zimbabwe, and Nigeria and Malawi are expected to follow soon) to protect intellectual property, and to ensure that writers, artists, photographers, or illustrators receive due remuneration for their creative work. He states that "on whatever level we attempt to develop a book policy, it should be founded on the understanding that respect for copyright encourages creativity."

2464

The Reproduction Rights Organization of Kenya/KOPIKEN. *Unauthorized Photocopying*. Nairobi: KOPIKEN [PO Box 31191], 1996. var. pp.

An information package put together by KOPIKEN, including its constitution and various documents setting out the organization's background and objectives, how it operates, funding requirements, etc. together with press clippings.

2465

United Nations Conference on Trade and Development/UNCTAD. *The TRIPS Agreement and Developing Countries*. New York and Geneva: United Nations (Sales no. 96.II.D.10), 1996. 64 pp.

The Trade Related Intellectual Property Rights (TRIPS), signed on 15 April 1994 in the framework of the Uruguay Round negations, represents an important change in international standards for protecting intellectual property in developing countries, and covers a wide range of disciplines. Following an introductory section on the main findings and conclusions, this study provides a detailed analysis of the implications of the TRIPS Agreement for developing economies. Copyright is discussed in section III, and examines the different areas of copyright protection relevant under TRIPS Agreement standards, the main implications, and implementation of protection, including that of computer programmes.

Educational and school book publishing

→ **See also: National book policies**
Teaching guides and texts

2466

Anon. "Réaliser des Ouvrages Bon Marché, c'est Possible." *AfriquEducation*, no. 13 (September 1995): 32-33.

Interview with Emmanuel Locha Mateso, head of ACCT's school book division, which discusses the development of the educational book publishing industry, and sets out the editorial policies of ACCT in this regard.

2467

Bo Sedin Consultants AB/ASG Transport Development *AB Study of the Distribution of Educational Materials in Tanzania. Final report 1993*. [Report by Bertil Dahlin] Stockholm [?]: Bo Sedin Consultants AB, 1993. [restricted circulation]

A distribution study that aimed to assist the Ministry of Education and Culture in Tanzania to overcome problems of distribution of educational materials in the country during a period of transition, i.e. whereby the previously state controlled production and distribution system is gradually making way for the private sector to take over the supply of educational materials. The study finds that the problems faced are not in fact distribution problems but are caused by problems of a financial and managerial/ organizational nature, and puts forward a series of short and long term recommendations how the situation might be improved.

2468

Chokpon, Comlan "Pénuries et Solutions d'Urgence." *AfriquEducation*, no. 13 (September 1995): 30-31.

Discusses the lamentable state of the school book publishing industry in most countries of Africa. Suggests that the only solution to this problem is to create regional publishing houses, which would entail the political will of African states to pool their resources and know-how.

2469

Commonwealth Secretariat. Women's and Youth Affairs Division *Gender Bias in School Text Books*. London: Commonwealth Secretariat [Marlborough House, Pall Mall, London SW1P 5HX], 1995. 96 pp.

In response to the lack of information on gender bias in existing textbooks in the countries of the Commonwealth, the Commonwealth Secretariat commissioned three major studies of primary school textbooks: one in the Caribbean, one in Asia, and one in Africa, the latter undertaken by Wanja Thairu (Kenya). The major findings of these studies are reported in this volume, which also includes further sections on 'Inclusive and gender sensitive language', 'Guidelines for textbook writers and producers', 'Suggestions for teachers and teacher educators', and the final section is an 'Evaluation guide' which presents a tool for the evaluation of gender bias in textbooks and other learning materials. Also includes a bibliography.

2470

< Ferns, Martin *National Seminar on Primary Textbook Publishing in Zambia: Report of an EMU/SIDA Seminar, Lusaka, 31 May and 1 June 1993.* Lusaka: Educational Materials Unit, Ministry of Education & Swedish International Development Agency, 1993 [?], 15 pp.

2471

Hymbound, Jean-Clotaire. "La Logique de la Banque Mondiale." *AfriquEducation*, no. 13 (September 1995): 34.

Examines the position of the World Bank on the issue of educational books in Africa and describes the 'Ille Project Education/RCA/IDA' which covers purchases of reading, science, and mathematics books for certain age groups of children. Whilst acknowledging the success of this project, it also questions the policy of giving books away free, as this will provide no guarantee for long term renewal, and is likely to upset a local book industry already hard hit by the recession.

2472

< International Institute for Educational Planning *Planning Textbook Development for Primary Education in Africa: report of an IIEP seminar*. Paris: International Institute for Educational Planning, 1992. 55 pp.

2473

McGregor, Charles "Doing it Better." *Bellagio Publishing Network Newsletter*, no. 18 (November 1996): 12.14

Asks what proportion of the world's textbook projects funded by international lenders and donors over the past ten years have failed, what caused these failures, and how can the failure rate be reduced. Presents a formula, the 'Epsilon index', by which success or failure of projects can be measured and scored.

2474

< United Nations Educational, Scientific, and Cultural Organisation. Regional Office for Education in Africa *Reducing the Cost of School Textbooks in Africa. Final report from a seminar*. Dakar: UNESCO BREDA/NEIDA, 1983. 71 pp.

2475

< United Nations Educational, Scientific, and Cultural Organisation "Dossier: textbook production in Third World countries." *Prospects* 13, no. 3 (1983): 315-369.

2476

< Zambia. Ministry of Education/Educational Materials Unit. *Zambia Educational Materials Project. Distribution Review*, by Arto Rissanen. Lusaka: Ministry of Education, Educational Materials Unit, 1993. 112 pp. [restricted circulation]

Examines the distribution problems of educational materials in the light of modern approaches in the areas of marketing, logistics and management, and the particular complexities of distribution of such materials in Zambia. Finds that there are several deficiencies in management action in terms of planning, implementation and control. Presents models for different parts of the distribution system and, through them, assesses the present and future roles of the government and private sector enterprises including printers, publishers, distributors and transporters. Concludes with a series of recommendations pin-pointing areas where potential and opportunities for improved performance exist.

2477

Zambia. Ministry of Education *Study on the Educational Materials Provision and Utilisation. Final report March 1995.* [Report prepared by NCG Sweden AB, in cooperation with the Vantaa Institute for Continuing Education, University of Helsinki]. Stockholm: SIDA/FINNIDA, 1995. var.pp. [restricted circulation]

Final report about the Zambia Educational Materials Project (ZEMP), an educational materials project which has enjoyed Nordic support since the mid 1980s but which is now being phased out. This study aims to determine the potential for development in the educational materials sector after the completion of ZEMP. Reviews the provision and financing of educational materials in Zambia, the state of the market, institutional structures, production capacity, utilization of educational materials, aspects of decentralization and external assistance, and concludes with a development scenario and a set of recommendations towards a sustainable system of supply of educational materials.

Intra-African book trade

→ See also: Bookselling and book distribution

2478

Ofori-Mensah, Akoss   *Marketing Books in Africa - A personal experience.* [Unpublished, photocopy; available from the Bellagio Publishing Network Secretariat, Oxford, 1995, 6 pp.]

> Paper presented to the Bellagio Publishing Network Round Table on Co-publishing, Addis Ababa, November 1995. A Ghanaian woman publisher looks at the problems and prospects of intra-African trading drawing on her own experience over a number of years "wandering about in Africa", and examines "what books can travel".

Journals and magazine publishing

2479

Adesokan, Akin   "Retelling a Forgettable Tale. *Black Orpheus* and *Transition* revisited." *Glendora Review* 1, no. 3 (1996): 49-57.

> Retells the story of the life and times of two of Africa's most exciting literary and cultural magazines: *Transition*, founded in Uganda by the late Rajat Neogy (and later published from Ghana where it was edited by Wole Soyinka as from 1974), and *Black Orpheus*, founded by Ulli Beier, Janheinz Jahn and Gerald Moore. Provides some insightful information about editorial policies, sources of funding, contributors to the journals, clashes of personality, and, in the case of *Transition*, clashes with the Obote government of the day who felt threatened by the journal's outspokenness. Concludes with a look at the 'new' *Transition* which, after a period of dormancy, has now recommenced publication from the USA.

2480

< African Association of Science Editors-Ethiopian Chapter *Proceedings of the Seminar on Managing and Editing Journals, 9-11 March 1993, IAR, Addis Ababa, Ethiopia*, edited by Damtew Teferra. Addis Ababa: African Association of Science Editors, Ethiopian Chapter, 1994. 76 pp.

> The fruits of a seminar on managing and editing journals, with synopses of the different presentations that were made and a record of the discussions that followed each presentation. The topics included editorial advisory boards, office management, communication with authors, copyright, manuscript tracking, ethics in scientific publishing, peer review, scientific and technical editing, and subscription management and distribution.

2481

Aina, L.O., and I.M. Mabawonku "Management of a Scholarly Journal in Africa: a success story." *African Journal of Library, Archives and Information Science* 6, no. 2 (1996): 63-84.

> An evaluation of the *African Journal of Library, Archives and Information Science* following five years of publication. Provides some background information about the journal's mission and goals, analyses the number of papers submitted for publication and their acceptance rate, and provides a detailed analysis of the number and type of subscribers and their country of origin. Also discusses some inhibiting factors affecting the journal's growth and development and day-to-day management, such as unreliable postal systems, high bank charges, foreign exchange constraints, and currency devaluations in Africa. Concludes that "with commitment and determination on the part of all the role players, a sustainable scholarly journal can be produced in Africa", but that its survival will largely depend on whether it will be able to attract a sufficient number of foreign subscriptions and therefore generate hard currency earnings.

2482

Beier, Ulli "Some Errors in the Article in Glendora no. 3." *Glendora Review* 1, no. 4 (1996): 8-9.

> A rejoinder to the Adesokan article (see entry 2479 above), in which Ulli Beier, former editor of *Black Orpheus* and co-founder of Mbari Club in Ibadan, sets the record straight and points out a number of inaccuracies in the Adesokan piece.

2483

Gibbs, Wayt W. "Lost Science in the Third World." *Scientific American* (August 1995): 76-83.

> Discusses the predicament of scientific journals in the developing world, who are trapped in a vicious circle of neglect, and bias: (i) articles are not cited because the journals have low visibility and are not well known, and because they are not included in the major citation databases and indexing/abstracting services. Or (ii) because the journal's peer review process is not of a sufficiently high standard, because the journal's limited accessibility discourages top scholars to act as referees; and (iii) domestic journals are unable to gain prestige and wide international circulation, because scholars from developing countries publish their best work with journals in the North because they feel domestic journals cannot adequately disseminate their work in the international academic community. The article also critically examines the power the Institute of Scientific Information (ISI) yields through its *Science Citation Index* in deciding what is 'worthy' of inclusion in their citation databases and what criteria must be met for inclusion of Third World journals.

2484

Glancey, Jonathan. "New Beat from Africa's Drummer". *The Independent* [London], (13 December 1995): 4-5.

> An interview with Jim Bailey founder, publisher, and editor-in-chief of *Drum*, Africa's first black magazine, which pioneered black African journalism.

2485

Huannou, Adrien. "Première Revue Scientifique et Littéraire du Bénin." *Notre Librairie*, no. 124 (October/December 1995): 35-39.

> An account of the early, influential, scholarly and literary review *La Reconnaissance Africaine*, which started publication in Benin (then Dahomey) in 1925; it later became *Etudes Dahoméennes*, but ceased publication in 1970 because of financial difficulties.

2486

Krieger, Milton "Building the Republic through Letters: *Abbia: Cameroun Cultural Review*, 1963-82, and its legacy." *Research in African Literatures* 27, no. 2 (Summer 1996): 153-177.

> Narrates the life of *Abbia*, a leading Cameroonian literary and cultural magazine that was founded by Bernard Fonlon in 1962, flourished in the 1960s, but then faltered in the late 1970s and finally lapsed in 1982 after publishing 40 volumes. It constituted "one of Africa's most prolific and comprehensive efforts to document and shape a national culture through the medium of the scholarly periodical." The article draws on interviews with some the surviving founders of the journal, examines contents, themes, and editorial policies over the years, and *Abbia*'s legacy and future bearings in Cameroon.

2487

Teferra, Damtew "Workshop for African Journal Editors." *Bellagio Publishing Network Newsletter*, no. 18 (November 1996): 5-6.

> Reports about a workshop organized by the International African Institute in Addis Ababa in May 1996, which aimed to assist editors of scientific and medical journals to improve their publishing operations, using the *Handbook of Good Practice in Journals Publishing* (see entry 2490) as the main working document, and which was put to the test during the workshop.

2488

Thomas, Ruth "Indexing African Journals." *African Publishing Review* 4, no. 6 (November/December 1995): 6.

> A report about the *Quarterly Index to Periodical Literature, Eastern and Southern Africa*, published by the Library of Congress Field Office in Nairobi since 1991, and which thus far has indexed almost 12,000 articles that have appeared in some 250 periodicals published in 24 African countries.

2489

Zell, Hans M. "African Journals in a Changing Environment of Scholarly Communication." In *APEX 96. African Periodicals Exhibit 1996*. Catalogue. Harare: Zimbabwe International Book Fair Trust; and London: Southern African Book Development Education Trust, 1996, 3-6.

> Changes of considerable magnitude are currently taking place in the academic and library communities, involving changes and advances in electronic technology, and behavioural changes within the academic community in accessing information through online electronic networks and through document delivery. Looks at the implications for African journal publishers, reviews serials acquisitions patterns and selection procedures in libraries, examines the bias by the world's major indexing and abstracting services and

online databases in not covering African serials, and offers some suggestions how African journals might survive in the electronic publishing age and prevent becoming marginalized even more.

2490

Zell, Hans M. *A Handbook of Good Practice in Journals Publishing.* London: International African Institute, pilot edition, 1996. 178 pp. (looseleaf format in A4 ring binder)

Aims to assist journal editors in Africa to improve their publishing operations by providing guidelines for good practice, and good housekeeping. Covers most aspects of journal publishing but puts emphasis on systems management, subscription fulfilment, and effective marketing and distribution. Includes a series of model guidelines and model forms that provide illustrative examples of good practice, together with a 'Resources' section (giving names and address of major subscription agents worldwide, resources for developing mailing lists, and details of major review and publicity outlets for African journals), and an annotated bibliography. Two specially commissioned contributions included as appendices cover 'Desktop publishing for beginners' by Roger Stringer, and 'Computerized subscription invoicing and fulfilment: some notes for small publishers' by David Brooks.

Libraries and publishing

→ See also: Acquisition of African-published material

2491

< Nwafor, B.V. "Problems of the Book Trade Infrastructure in Developing Countries in Relation to University Libraries Objectives." *IFLA Journal* 10, no. 4 (1984): 357-368.

2492

Zeleza, Paul Tiyambe "Manufacturing and Consuming Knowledge. African libraries and publishing." *Development in Practice* 6, no. 4 (November 1996): 293-303.

Examines the problems facing African scholars, publishers, and libraries in the context of rapid developments in information technology, a deepening economic gulf between industrialized and Third World countries, and a continuing dependency on Western forms of knowledge and systems to validate all forms of intellectual activity. The author calls on the scholarly community in Africa to reclaim African studies: "importing knowledge from abroad is no panacea. And for Africa to depend on external sources for knowledge about itself is a cultural and an economic travesty of monumental proportions." The real challenge is "not simply to fill empty library shelves and acquire gadgets for faster information retrieval, but to produce the knowledge in the first place." Also examines the challenges, and constraints, of publishing in Africa, and argues that "libraries must do their part" and "having fed for so long on Western imports and donations of information materials and technologies, African libraries have not always ventured with enough appetite to acquire local publications." In his conclusion the author questions the terms 'information-rich' and 'information poor', and stresses the needs for Africans to develop the means to generate, value, and effectively disseminate their own forms of knowledge.

Mass market and popular literature publishing

2493

< Russell, Terry, and Steve Murray *Popular Publishing for Environmental and Health Education: Evaluation of Action Magazine.* Liverpool: Liverpool University Press, 1993. 242 pp.

Action Magazine is a non-government donor-funded project based in Harare, which produces a magazine for schools targeted at top primary level using a 'popular publishing' format - with comic book elements, fun and games features, cartoons, etc. - to present health and environmental science material in a manner which is attractive and easily accessible to children. The magazine is being distributed to every school in Zimbabwe, and, more recently, to some other countries in the Southern African region. This evaluation examined the use of the magazine in Zimbabwe and in Botswana. Issues included children's visual literacy and appreciation of the health education messages, as well as the broader impact of health and environment science information on schools, children and the wider community, especially the remote and disadvantaged rural communities.

Multinational publishers in Africa

2494

Apeji, Eric Adeche *The Contributions of Multinational Publishers to the Provision of Books in Nigeria* [Unpublished, Ph.D. thesis, University of Ibadan, 1995]

National book policies

→   **See also: Book development councils**
       Educational and school book publishing
       State participation in publishing

2495

Aina, Take Akin "Book Policy and Information Objectives: some reflections on relationships and problems." In *National Book Policies for Africa*, edited by Murray McCartney. Harare: Zimbabwe International Book Fair Trust, 1996, 66-70.

Argues that it is necessary to question the notion of book policy and information objectives - and the assumptions and practices they embody - and first ask the broader and troublesome questions: Whose books? Whose policies? Whose information? Whose objectives? "We cannot talk about policies and national objectives without remembering the grim existence of systematic polarization and exclusion, extensive inequality, and in some cases barbaric domination and exploitation."

2496

Coulibaly, N'Golo "The Role of the Education Sector in National Book Policy: management or facilitation?" In *National Book Policies for Africa*, edited by Murray McCartney. Harare: Zimbabwe International Book Fair Trust, 1996, 27-29.

Describes the emergence of a national book policy in Mali and states that "education for all cannot be realized without a national book development policy for books written in both national and foreign languages."

2497

Evans, Nicholas "National Book Policy in South Africa: catching up with other countries." In *National Book Policies for Africa*, edited by Murray McCartney. Harare: Zimbabwe International Book Fair Trust, 1996, 38-40.

Identifies some of the fundamental questions that will need to be addressed before a viable book awareness campaign, and an effective national book policy, can take off in South Africa.

2498

Garzón, Alvaro "National Book Policy." [Unpublished, photocopy; available from UNESCO, Book and Copyright Division, Paris, 1996, 24 pp.]

Paper presented to the Interregional Meeting of Book Promotion Networks/ INTERBOOK, Paris, May 22-24, 1996. Examines why so many initiatives aimed at encouraging the production and distribution of books in developing countries have failed. Thereafter analyses the major objectives of a national book policy, and the various subsectors concerned (i.e. author, publisher, printer, distributor, and the reader/libraries.) States that "a detailed assessment of the situation in each sub-sector is the real basis on which to build a national book policy" and that such an assessment should then reveal the principal deficiencies in each subsector. Also looks at "the machinery of book development", i.e. the policies and strategies that should govern the work of the various professions related to the book sector, and the factors that should be considered in assessing the state of each sector. Finally, provides some guidelines for those working in the field of book policy strategy and describes one of the approaches used in the implementation of national book policies, namely that of the Latin America and the Caribbean (CERLAL) UNESCO programme.

2499

Ike, Chukwuemeka "The Relationship Between State, Private and NGO Development Sectors in Book Policy Formulation." In *National Book Policies for Africa*, edited by Murray McCartney. Harare: Zimbabwe International Book Fair Trust, 1996, 21-27.

The Director of the Nigerian Book Foundation, examines the role of the three key players in book development and the formation of a national book policy: the state, the private sector, and NGOs. He warns that there will be serious problems in leaving national book policy formation entirely in state hands, and that experience had shown that government concern for book development has been largely limited to textbook development. The private sector tends to be more preoccupied with showing a healthy balance sheet, and their concern for authorship "is confined to organizing workshops for the production of school textbooks, and few of them pay more than lip service to the problems of national or indigenous book development." NGOs, on the other hand, have no monetary interest in the book industry and no shareholders to keep happy, and they are therefore able to take a detached, comprehensive, and holistic view of the problems of national book development.

2500

Kromberg, Steve "Developing a Book Policy for South Africa." In *National Book Policies for Africa*, edited by Murray McCartney. Harare: Zimbabwe International Book Fair Trust, 1996, 37-38.

Describes some of the prerequisites for a successful book development policy for South Africa.

2501

McCartney, Murray (ed.) *National Book Policies for Africa. The Key to Long-Term Development. Proceedings of the Zimbabwe International Book Fair Indaba 1996, Harare, Zimbabwe, 26-27 July 1996.* Harare: Zimbabwe International Book Fair Trust, 1996. 84 pp.

The proceedings of an 'Indaba' on national book policies held immediately before the 1996 Zimbabwe International Book Fair, and which attracted participants and speakers from many parts of Africa and elsewhere, representing the whole spectrum of book sector interests. Conceived in collaboration with the Association for the Development of African Education (ADAE) Working Group on Books and Learning Materials, the 'Indaba' deliberated extensively on the desirability of effective instruments to promote the development of the African book industries. A National Book Policy "was recognized as constituting the basic framework within which the legitimate interests of all actors and stakeholders in book-related industries are recognized, and they are empowered to contribute towards the creation of a book reading democratic society." (Note: most papers in the volume are individually abstracted; see individual entries in this section and elsewhere)

2502

Nwankwo, Victor "Inter-sectoral Co-ordination in the Book Industry: the publishing sub-sector." In *National Book Policies for Africa*, edited by Murray McCartney. Harare: Zimbabwe International Book Fair Trust, 1996, 58-61.

States that the need for a national book policy is now well recognized and no longer an issue for debate, but that "translating this recognition into an effective policy is a burning concern." Examines various initiatives towards a coherent national book policy in Nigeria and the roles played by the Nigerian Book Development Council and, more recently, by the Nigerian Book Foundation. Concludes that Nigeria's national book policy still lacks the enabling book legislation "necessary to bring it to practical usefulness, but it has come a long way."

2503

Omotoso, Kole "The Literate Environment: its relationship to national development." In *National Book Policies for Africa*, edited by Murray McCartney. Harare: Zimbabwe International Book Fair Trust, 1996, 9-12.

> A keynote address, by a prominent Nigerian writer, presented at the 'Indaba' on national book policies. Deplores the lack of vision by African governments, their failure to create a literate environment, and states that there is a need for the creation of a community which cherishes fundamental moral values: "We cannot have national book policies if we do not have personal book policies. We cannot create a national literate environment if such an environment does not exist in our immediate surroundings. There can be no national development if there is no individual development."

2504

Priestley, Carol, and Carew Treffgarne "Zimbabwe Book Fair Activities: National Book Policy Indaba and DAE Working Group Meetings." *Bellagio Publishing Network Newsletter*, no. 18 (November 1996): 3-4.

> Reports about an 'Indaba' on "National Book Policy: the key to long-term book development", a two-day programme held immediately before the 1996 Zimbabwe International Book Fair, and organized in collaboration with the Association for the Development of Education in Africa (DAE) [now ADEA] Working Group on Books an Learning Materials. The 'Indaba' explored the connections between national book policy and national development, and national cultural policy. The question of publishing materials in national languages emerged as one of the dominant themes. (See entry 2501 for the 'Indaba' proceedings).

2505

Walter, Scott; Diana Newton, and Paul Osborn "National Book Sector Outlines." [Unpublished, photocopy; available from UNESCO, Book and Copyright Division, Paris, 1996, 11 pp, +11 pp. appendix]

> Discussion paper prepared for the International Meeting of Book Promotion Networks/INTERBOOK, Paris, May 22-24, 1996. Describes a model for the preparation of national book sector outlines, intended to provide a "snapshot" of the current state of the book and the publishing industries in any country, and quick access to relevant and up-to-date information. Sets out the proposed classification system of headings and sub-headings for the outlines, and, in an appendix, gives a sample national book sector outline, using Mali as an example.

Noma Award for Publishing in Africa

2506

Noma Award Managing Committee. *The Noma Award for Publishing in Africa. Winners, special commendations and honourable mentions, 1990-1995*. Oxford: The Noma Award for Publishing in Africa [Noma Award Secretariat, PO Box 128, Witney, OX8 5XU, UK], 1995. 12 pp.

> Updated brochure giving details of Noma Award winners, special commendations, and honourable mentions for 1990-1995, with jury citations, etc. Also includes a complete list of winners for 1980-1989.

2507

"The Noma Award for Publishing in Africa." *Southern African Review of Books*, no. 41 (January-February 1996): 18-19.

> For the first time in the Noma Award's history, the annual Award ceremony took place in South Africa, in February 1996. The winner of the 1995 prize was Marlene van Niekerk for her novel in Afrikaans *Triomf*, and which was also the first time that a book written in Afrikaans had won the Award. This is a selection of the speeches given at the ceremony, including those by Chair of the Noma Award Committee, Walter Bgoya, and the Award winner's speech.

2508

Zell, Hans M. "A Sixteen-year Japanese Contribution to African Publishing." *Logos* 7, no. 2 (1996): 162-167 [Appendix 2 & 3 in this article published in *Logos* 7, no. 3 (1996): 245-246]

> The former Secretary of the Noma Award for Publishing looks back at the accomplishments of the Award since its inception in 1979. He sets out the background that led to the establishment of the Award, the vision of the Award's sponsor the late Shoichi Noma, the categories in which books may be submitted for the prize, and the working methods of the Noma Award jury and secretariat, which is assisted by a pool of almost 300 assessors and subject authorities from throughout the world. Also reflects on the Noma Award's relationship with African books, the exposure that has been given over the years to a wide spectrum of African writing and scholarship, and the success it has achieved in its main mission to promote publishing in Africa. Three appendixes include a complete list of winners from 1980-1995; an analysis of Award winners by nationality, gender, language of publication, and categories; and a Noma Award publisher's 'League Table'.

Printing industries and the graphic arts/Manufacturing

→ See also: Pulp and paper industries

2509

Jegede, S.A.O., and N.A. Njoku "Local Production of Ink for the Book Industry." In *Making Books Available and Affordable*, edited by Ezenwa-Ohaeto. Awka, Nigeria: Nigerian Book Foundation, 1995, 55-63.

> Defines the nature of ink and paper supplies for the book industries and looks at the development and growth of the ink industry in Nigeria and the efforts made by both manufacturers and the government to meet local demand. Examines the numerous constraints facing the industry and makes some suggestions on a possible way forward. Argues that the importation of finished ink should be banned by the government, or taxed heavily, to protect local ink industries.

2510

Nyamangara, William   "Inter-sectorial Co-ordination in the Book Industry: the printing sub-sector." In *National Book Policies for Africa*, edited by Murray McCartney. Harare: Zimbabwe International Book Fair Trust, 1996, 62-63.

> A printer's perspective on the debate about national book policies, who states that printers are often asked to provide 'first world' standards at 'third world' prices. Briefly describes some of the difficulties faced by the book production industries who, like publishers, are operating in a harsh economic climate, and makes a number of suggestions how the situation might be improved.

2511

< Odiadi, Austin "Printing Development in Nigeria 1980-1990." *Nigerian Printer* 4, no. 4 (1990): 21-22.

2512

Odufua, Tunde "Local Production of Plates, Chemicals and other Materials for the Book Industry." In *Making Books Available and Affordable*, edited by Ezenwa-Ohaeto. Awka, Nigeria: Nigerian Book Foundation, 1995, 64-76.

> Starts off with an overview of the major printing processes and the most economical processes for book production, and thereafter reviews local production (in Nigeria) of lithographic plates and light-sensitive materials for making plates, as well as materials required for finishing and binding in the book manufacturing process. Calls for more research organizations in Nigeria that could aid the needs of the printing and publishing industries.

Publishing, of African writers and African literature (and Publishing about Africa)

→   **See also: Authors and publishers/The role of the writer**

2513

Chakava, Henry "Publishing Ngugi: the challenge, the risk and the reward. With an appendix on useful references on Ngugi's work." *Matatu*, nos. 15/16 (1996): 183-200.

> Reprint of an article published in 1994; for annotation see entry 2030 in main bibliography.

2514

Whiteman, Kaye "Publishing about Africa." *West Africa*, no. 4123 (4-10 November 1996): 1712-1713.

> Reports about the publishing activities of Hans Zell Publishers, and about Hans Zell's past work for the Oxford-based African Books Collective, and as Secretary to the Noma Award for Publishing in Africa Managing Committee.

Pulp and paper industries

→   **See also: Printing industries and the graphic arts/Manufacturing**

2515

Shoyinka, S.A. "The Book Industry and Local Production of Long Fibre." In *Making Books Available and Affordable*, edited by Ezenwa-Ohaeto. Awka, Nigeria: Nigerian Book Foundation, 1995, 40-44.

> Nigeria has three paper mills, but one of these is yet to come on stream, and the two functional mills currently operate at only 50% of capacity due to a lack of long fibre pulping materials, caused in turn by escalating costs and the dramatic decline of the Naira. Examines Kenaf (*Hibiscus cannabinus* L), a non-woody pulp, as an alternative to imported long fibre pulp, its potential as a source of high quality long fibre in the manufacture of pulp and paper, and the production of Kenaf production in Nigeria. Points out however that "the greatest constraint affecting Kenaf production in the country has been lack of recognition of the immense importance of this crop, hence inadequate government support for its promotion." Believes that the remarkable progress made in the culture of non-woody long fibre sources such as Kenaf in the USA, Thailand, and Australia could be replicated in Nigeria.

Reading habit and reading promotion

→   **See also: Children's book publishing
Libraries and publishing**

2516

Anon. "Taking Reading to New Heights." *Kalulu News* 7, no. 3 (October 1995): 1-2.

> Describes the success of the 'Children's Reading Tent', a special attraction at the annual Pan-African Children's Book Fair held in Nairobi, and which was created to provide "a near ideal setting in which children can read books of their choice at their own pace."

2517

Bugembe, Mary "The Children's Reading Tent." *African Publishing Review* 5, no. 2 (March/April 1996): 1-2.

> Reports about a mobile children's reading tent, an innovative idea being experimented with by the Council for the Promotion of Children's Science Publications in Africa (CHISCI), and analyses the public's and children's response to this activity.

2518

Heale, Jay "So What do Young Readers Want to Read?" *African Publishing Review* 4, no. 6 (November/December 1995): 14.

> Argues that children's opinions are important and that children (in South Africa) should have a right to decide for themselves what they want to read, rather than having books imposed on them which are officially 'approved' or 'prescribed' by educational bodies. Calls for a well-endowed children's book award decided on by panels of the children themselves, along the lines of the Smarties Prize in the UK.

2519

< Leach, Athol, and Jennifer Verbeek "The Reading Habits of Adults in Anglophone Sub-Saharan Africa: A historical overview." *African Journal of Library, Archives & Information Science* 3, no. 2 (October 1993) 95-106.

2520

Milliken, Phoebe "How to Make Children Sit Quietly for Long Periods of Time: lessons from the children's reading tent at the Zimbabwe International Book Fair." *African Publishing Review* 5, no. 6 (November/December 1996): 10-11.

> Reports about reactions of children to activities and readings taking place at a reading tent that was part of a series of book promotional events held during the Zimbabwe Book Fair. Found that most children preferred to read the glossier imported books with plentiful illustrations, rather than locally-produced children's books, the vast majority of which were easy readers with rather narrow appeal. Urges local publishers to become more committed to the children's market by allocating more resources to the production of creative texts and picture-story books that are visually appealing.

2521

< Osanyin, Bode "Cultivating a Reading Public - a way to Nigerian identity." *Nigeria Magazine* 57, no. 3/4 (1989): 68-75.

2522

Radebe, Thuli "Reading Interests of Zulu-speaking Standard Two Children in Pietermaritzburg." *South African Journal of Library and Information Science* 63, no. 4 (December 1995): 161-172.

> A study conducted in response to the need, expressed by parents, teachers, information workers, and publishers, for information and guidance regarding the reading interests of black children in South Africa. A sample of children's books was selected and presented to a group of children to test their interests. The study found that children did not necessarily prefer settings and situations which were familiar to their own circumstances; they did not necessarily select books which were written in an African language (i.e. Zulu); reading emerged as an individual matter regardless of ethnicity or race; and children's preferences had no significant relationship to the ethnic origin of the story.

2523

Sagna, R. "Popular Reading in Francophone sub-Saharan Africa." In *Proceedings of the Seminar on Information Provision to Rural Communities in Africa*, held in Gaborone, Botswana, 22-25 June, 1994, edited by Eve Johansson. Gaborone: Botswana National Library Services; and Uppsala: Department of Non-Formal Education, Uppsala University Library, 1995, 17-20.

> Discusses the role and promotion of popular reading in francophone Africa through the establishment of national networks for reading in urban, semi rural and rural communities. Focuses on the role played by the Centre de Lecture et d'Animation Culturelle (CLAC) schemes and experiments.

2524

Staunton, Irene " 'Sorry, no Free Reading'." In *Africa Bibliography 1994*, compiled by Christopher H. Allen. Edinburgh: Edinburgh University Press, 1995, vi-xi.
[Also published in *African Research and Documentation*, no. 69 (1995): 17-22]

> The Publishing Director of Baobab Books in Harare describes the provision of textbooks and other reading materials to children in Zimbabwe from the period immediately following independence until the current situation today. She finds that most school children's experience of books is often a negative one and sets out some of the reasons why this is so. She also cites a number of recent developments and initiatives which might lead to an improvement of the situation in the future, and states that "if people are given access to books that they want to read, and if they are encouraged to see books as providing more than a source of information which must be learned for an examination, the potential for developing a more broadly based reading culture is promising."

2525

Zawua, J. "Promoting Reading Among Children in Nigeria." *African Journal of Library, Archives and Information Science* 6, no. 2 (1996), 107-112.

Rights sales, licensing and co-publishing

→ **See also: Copyright**

2526

Altbach, Philip G. "Co-publishing: benefits and costs." *Bellagio Publishing Network Newsletter*, no. 16 (Spring 1996): 2-3.
[Also published in *African Publishing Review* 5, no. 2 (March/April 1996): 14-15.]

> Reports on a Bellagio Group sponsored seminar held in Addis Ababa in November 1995, which focused on co-publishing with special emphasis on its relevance for Africa. Participants discussed both North-South and South-South collaboration - and examined possible models - but found that at this time there is only limited collaboration among African publishers in different countries.

2527

Brickhill, Paul *Some Ideas Related to South-North Co-publications.* [Unpublished, photocopy; available from the Bellagio Publishing Network Secretariat, Oxford, 1995, 7 pp.]

> Paper presented to the Bellagio Publishing Network Round Table on Co-publishing, Addis Ababa, November 21-22, 1995. Assesses the prospects of joint ventures with overseas partners new to Africa; partnerships with small-scale foreign publishers; and partnerships with NGO publishers. States that co-publishing "offers African book development a means of accelerating sustainable, viable publishing projects on a scale not previously accessible to most commercial publishers."

2528

Chakava, Henry *Inter-African Co-publishing.* [Unpublished, photocopy; available from the Bellagio Publishing Network Secretariat, Oxford, 1995, 5 pp.]

Paper presented to the Bellagio Publishing Network Round Table on Co-publishing, Addis Ababa, November 21-22, 1995. Outlines some of the critical issues and factors that need to be addressed to facilitate more effective co-operation in African publishing and a flourishing intra-African book trade.

2529

Chakava, Henry "Publishing Partnerships between Africa and the North: a dream or a possibility?"
Bellagio Publishing Network Newsletter, no. 15 (November 1995): 4-6.
Examines the prospects of more equitable partnerships and joint ventures between publishers in Africa and those in the North. Argues that "the best way to end state publishing in Africa and stop its future recurrence is for the Northern publishers to support commercial publishing and thereby help to create credible partners with whom they can trade in the future."

2530

Kor, Buma *The African Co-publishing Programme at the Regional Centre for Book Promotion in Africa (CREPLA), Yaoundé, Cameroon.* [Unpublished, photocopy; available from the Bellagio Publishing Network Secretariat, Oxford, 1995, 5 pp.]
Paper presented to the Bellagio Publishing Network Round Table on Co-publishing, Addis Ababa, November 21-22, 1995. Provides the background about a CREPLA/UNESCO initiated African co-publishing programme launched in 1979, examines some of the reasons why it failed, and the lessons to be learnt from this failure.

2531

Kumar, Arvind "Co-publication Models." [Unpublished, photocopy; available from UNESCO, Book and Copyright Division, Paris, 1996, 12 pp.]
Discussion paper prepared for the Interregional Meeting of Book Promotion Networks/INTERBOOK, Paris, May 22-24, 1996. The Director of the National Book Trust in India sets out some of the current practices for co-publication, drawing mainly on the experience in India but also looking at the Asia/Pacific Co-publication Programme co-ordinated with the support of UNESCO, and the experience of the Columbia-based Latin American Co-publication Programme. In addition to South-South partnerships, the paper reviews possible co-publication models for North-South and South-North ventures, and the feasibility of developing an African co-publication programme.

2532

McCartney, Murray *APNET Seminar: Intra-African Rights Trading. Harare 31 July 1995.* Harare: APNET, *African Publishing Review* Supplement, 1995. 11 pp.
The summary report of an APNET seminar on intra-African rights trading. Includes a list of delegates.

2533

Nwankwo, Victor "Publishing Partnerships Between Africa and the North. A Dream or a Possibility?" *African Publishing Review* 5, no. 3 (May/June 1996): 6-7.
[Also published in *Bellagio Publishing Network Newsletter*, no. 18 (November 1996): 18-19]

Another perspective on North/South partnerships (see also entry 2529 by Chakava above). Reports about a meeting on North/South publishing cooperation held during the Frankfurt Book Fair in 1995. Outlines the main factors that come into play in publishing partnerships between African publishers and those in the North, and examines the case of one ongoing partnership between New Namibia Books and Heinemann Educational Publishers. Concludes that "sufficient experience in on-going collaborations exist to make it possible to identify characteristics on which to build models for future cooperation."

2534

Singh, Tejeshwar *South-South Co-publishing.* [Unpublished, photocopy; available from the Bellagio Publishing Network Secretariat, Oxford, 1995, 11 pp.]

Paper presented to the Bellagio Publishing Network Round Table on Co-publishing, Addis Ababa, November 1995. A perspective on South-South co-publishing by a prominent Indian publisher. Proposes, and critically examines, three basic models of co-publishing which might work in an African context.

Scholarly publishing (General)

→   **See also: Scientific, technical and medical publishing**

2535

Aina, Tade Akin "Social Science Scholarly Publishing in Africa: the CODESRIA experience." *Focus on International and Comparative Librarianship* 26, no. 2 (September 1995): 72-78.

[Also published in *African Research and Documentation,* no. 69 (1995): 23-27]

Describes the book and journals publishing programme of the Council for the Development of Social Science Research in Africa (CODESRIA) based in Dakar, Senegal. Examines some of the constraints faced by scholarly publishers in Africa, "hindered by problems of distribution, and linguistic, political, cultural and fiscal barriers", and sets out how CODESRIA has tackled these problems. Also reports about CODESRIA's attempts to provide more visibility for their books in the major academic libraries in the North.

2536

Bankole, Bodunde   "Scholarly Publishing. The University of Lagos Press Experiences: constraints and the way forward." [Unpublished, photocopy; available from APNET, Harare, 1996, 9 pp.]

Paper presented to an APNET Seminar on Scholarly Publishing, Accra, November 5-6, 1996. The Director of the University of Lagos Press describes the development of this press, which has grown from a conventional university press governed by an academic Publications Committee of the university into a self-accounting entity, and run as a business arm of the university since 1990. However, publishing activities have been severely curtailed because of the economic decline of the country, rampant inflation, political instability, and dramatic disruption of university life. Also describes other constraints such as low-level manufacturing standards, unreliable postal services, poor retail outlets, impoverished libraries, and other factors. Makes a number of macro- and micro-level recommendations on a possible way forward to revive scholarly publishing output in Nigeria.

2537

Fatokun, Akin "Publishing Activities at the Obafemi Awolowo University Press, Ile-Ife: problems and prospects." [Unpublished, photocopy; available from APNET, Harare, 1996, 12 pp.]

Paper delivered at an APNET Seminar on Scholarly Publishing, Accra, November 5-6, 1996. Describes the experience of a Nigerian university press which, since 1980, has been operating as an autonomous self-accounting unit of the university, as a private limited company wholly owned by the university. Provides an account of the press's structure, editorial list development, promotion and sales activities, and examines current problems in the areas of manuscript acquisitions, book manufacturing, marketing, the illegal copying of books, bad debts, and the special problems created by the dramatic drop in the purchasing power of the Naira. Also pleads for more positive support by Nigerian university authorities for its scholarly presses, and describes some examples of university bureaucracy and shocking waste of funds: in 1980 the Nigerian National Universities Commission (NUC) allocated a sum of 3 million Naira to Obafemi Awolowo University to help it set up a medium-sized printshop, which was to be become operational within a period of one year. However the university-appointed building contractors took nine years to complete the work, and by which time any remaining funds for printing presses or origination equipment had been eaten up by escalating costs and inflation. The result was, "that the Press was unable to buy one single item of printing equipment and so the Naira 3m. was lost to bureaucracy. Today, we are starting all over again."

2538

Field-Juma, Alison "Initiative in Scholarly Publishing." *Innovation* [Nairobi] 4, no. 1 (July 1996): 4-5.

A brief profile of Initiatives Ltd., in Nairobi, a company founded in 1988 to produce and publish technical and scholarly books, and which has worked in close collaboration with the African Centre for Technology Studies (ACTS).

2539

Jaygbay, Jacob "Self-censorship and African Scholarship. Implications for scholarly publishing." *Bellagio Publishing Network Newsletter*, no. 18 (November 1996): 14-17.

Is concerned with a form of censorship that "take place within the academic community itself, those imposed by the structure and content of education, and those emanating from societal pressures." Examines how this affects scholarly knowledge production, data collection in the social sciences, choice of language, together with the constraints of societal pressures, and states that "African scholars as well as scholarly publishers do not help the situation by failing to present a true picture of what goes on in African societies in the hope of remaining in business."

2540

Jaygbay, Jacob "Scholarly Publishing in Francophone Africa." *The African Book Publishing Record* 22, no. 2, (1996): 99-105.

Focuses on the production and dissemination of scholarly communication in Africa with special emphasis on francophone countries. Special attention is given to issues relating to the transfer of knowledge from one language to another; the nature of African scholarship and the constraints under which African academics currently work; the reading culture of Africans and stereotype views and assumptions relating to the reading habit; the impact of the new technologies and electronic publishing; the production, distribution, promotion of scholarly publishing output; and the emerging trends in financing scholarly publishing in Africa. Concludes that "publishers, scholars and creative writers who want to reach the African public should go beyond unproven assumptions" regarding the reading habit, and "must become more 'market oriented' by striving to understand the reading needs of the African readership, how these needs are expressed, and how they can be met by more innovative approaches."

2541

Katama, Agnes   "Environet. One Step Towards Self-Sustaining Publishing of Environmental and Agricultural Studies in Africa." *CASP News Digest* 1, no. 2 (July 1996): 3-4.

Reports about the work and objectives of the Environmental Publishing Network (ENVIRONET) established at the International Centre of Insect Physiology and Ecology in Nairobi, which aims to develop strategies for a financially self-sustaining operation publishing environmental material for the tertiary reading level, and to effectively disseminate this material and research findings. Six institutions are currently part of the network.

2542

Katama, Agnes "Management and Business Premises within the Context of a Self-Financing Scholarly Publishing Press: the case of ICIPE Science Press (ISP)." [Unpublished, photocopy; available from APNET, Harare, 1996, 10 pp.]

Paper presented to an APNET Seminar on Scholarly Publishing, Accra, November 6-8, 1996. Describes the mandate and raison d' être of the Nairobi-based ICIPE Science Press established in 1988, and its structure, finance and operations. Apart from serving the publishing needs of the International Centre for Insect Physiology and Ecology, the Press also undertakes/coordinates publishing projects for other academic institutions, and through this generates extra income. Although currently donor-supported, the Press aims to become financially independent by the end of 1997. The paper outlines the steps that are being taken to increase self-generated income and achieving self-sufficiency. Suggests that the ISP model for self-sustainability could be adopted by scholarly publishers and research institutions in other parts of Africa.

2543

Katama, Agnes "Resource Sharing, Marketing and Self-Sustainability in Africa: ENVIRONET-towards a model for resource sharing in Africa's tertiary readership." *African Research and Documentation*, no. 69 (1995): 28-29.

Calls for more sharing of resources and expertise among Africa's scholarly publishers to lessen their dependence on donor funding.

2544

Kiboi, Muthui "Scholarly Publishing in Kenya." [Unpublished, photocopy; available from APNET, Harare, 1996, 8 pp.]

Paper presented to an APNET Seminar on Scholarly Publishing, Accra, November 5-6, 1996. Presents an overview of the publishing industry in Kenya, and scholarly publishing in particular, and analyzes "the extent to which various factors have hindered or helped publishers to be able to deal with the challenges of publishing or attempting to publish in this field." Finds that many publishers, in addition to being reluctant to publish territory-level books because of high editorial development costs, feel uneasy to handle manuscripts of a technical nature. Identifies training of African trainers as one of the most pressing problems. Calls for more co-publishing projects between African academic and scholarly publishers, as well as improved relationships between authors, institutions and publishers.

2545

Michira, Christine "Consortium for African Scholarly Publishing: an idea long overdue." *Innovation* [Nairobi] 4, no. 1 (July 1996): 8-9.

A Kenyan law student welcomes the establishment of the Consortium for African Scholarly Publishing (CASP), and believes it has an important role to play in promoting African scholarship.

2546

Nwabera, Alice "Capacity Development and Increasing Production of Scholarly Publications." *Innovation* [Nairobi] 4, no. 1 (July 1996): 3.

A brief account of the aims and objectives of the Nairobi-based Consortium of African Scholarly Publishers (CASP).

2547

Nyambura, Joyce "CASP Aims High for Publishers and Scholars." *Innovation* [Nairobi] 4, no. 1 (July 1996): 12-13.

An interview with Elizabeth Larson, Co-ordinator of the Consortium of African Scholarly Publishers (CASP), in which she sets out some of the objectives of the organization and its plans for the future.

2548

Shaba, Steve "Flogging a Dead Horse? The state of tertiary book publishing in Nigeria." *Glendora Review* 1, no. 3 (1996): 39-41.

Takes stock of the tertiary publishing crisis in Nigeria; finds that it is "comatose", and offers a number of strategies and suggestions which the author believes will improve the current situation "with or without a depressed economy".

Scientific, technical and medical publishing

→   **See also: Scholarly publishing (General)**

2549

< Ethiopian Science and Technology Commission *Profile of Science and Technology Publications in Ethiopia.* Addis Ababa: Ethiopian Science and Technology Commission, Science and Technology Popularization Department [PO Box 2490], 1994. 39 pp.

2550

Isoun, T.T. "Publishing and Productivity of Science in Africa: Scientometrics." *Whydah* 5, no. 1 (March 1996): 1-4.

> Looks at funding of scientific research in Africa, criteria for measuring productivity of sciences, and provides a short overview of the current state of science and technology research in Africa. Reviews the activities of Academy Science Publishers in Nairobi, including its journal *Discovery and Innovation.* States that despite the fact that some progress has been made by African publishers, the publication of scientific and scholarly works in Africa is still "beset with a multiplicity of problems and constraints", and calls on African governments and development institutions to provide more encouragement and positive support to the African book industries.

2551

Teferra, Damtew "The Status and Capacity of Science Publishing in Africa." *Journal of Scholarly Publishing* 27, no. 1 (October 1995): 28-36.

> Assesses the state of scientific publishing and, in particular, attempts to assess the scientific research published by individual countries of Africa on the basis of an analysis of data from the *Scientific Citation Index* (published by the Institute of Scientific Information/ISI) between 1981 to 1993. Compares the position of and the trends in science publishing in individual African countries, and by region. Finds that most of the publications are in the life sciences, especially agriculture and health, and that publishing output in the physical sciences is still very small. The analysis also showed that output in some of the largest producers, such as Nigeria, has declined; in other countries, such as Kenya and Morocco, it has increased dramatically.

State participation in publishing

→   **See also: National book policies**

2552

Altbach, Philip G. (ed.) *The Challenge of the Market: privatization and publishing in Africa.* Chestnut Hill, MA: Bellagio Publishing Network Research and Information Center, (Bellagio Studies in Publishing, 7), 1996. 114 pp.

This collection of papers focuses on the transition from state to private sector publishing in Africa. Two overview evaluations draw attention to the fact that the road to privatization is not necessarily an easy one, and that there are costs as well as benefits involved. Four cases studies, from Ghana, Ethiopia, Zambia and the Côte d'Ivoire (all individually listed/abstracted elsewhere in this volume), provide accounts of specific experiences. For contrast, and comparative purposes, the volume also includes a chapter assessing the prospects for private publishing in the central Asian republics of the former Soviet Union.

Training for book industry personnel

2553
African Publishers' Network/African Publishing Institute *African Publishing Institute's Curriculum*. Harare, APNET, and Nairobi: African Publishing Institute, Regional Office, [PO Box 31191, Nairobi], 1996. 39 pp. [photocopied]
> The African Publishing Institute (API) was established by APNET to co-ordinate and initiate training for the African publishing industry. In pursuit of its training goals, API has now completed formation of a curriculum for training designed to meet the training needs for all professional levels within the industry. This document sets out the structure of the curriculum, with some of the courses split into modules according to the nature of their objects and contents. The duration of courses, which includes a foundation course, range from one to five days.

2554
Bedingfield, Margo "API's Publishing Training Curriculum." *African Publishing Review* 5, no. 5 (September/October) 1996: 1-2.
> A brief report about a meeting held in Kenya in May 1996 that was convened with the goal of evaluating APNET's training activities to date, and that established an official African Publishing Institute (API) training curriculum which will form the basis of future API training programmes (see also entry 2553).

2555
Irura, Stanley "Training for African Publishers. An Overview of Some Initiatives." [Unpublished, photocopy; available from CODE Europe, Oxford, 5 pp.]
> Paper presented to a CODE Europe seminar on The Commercial Development of African Publishing, Oxford, April 11-12, 1996. Presents an overview of training opportunities currently available for the African book professions, including workshops and courses initiated by APNET's African Publishing Institute (API), and training available at some academic institutions. Briefly examines some of the problems and constraints in the further development of the API programme.

2556
Tettey, Edem *Developing Human Resources of the Book Industry in West Africa. A Decade of Promoting Professionalism in African Publishing: a review and evaluation of the Ghana project*. Kumasi, Ghana: Department of Book Industry, College of Arts, University of Science and Technology, 1996. 14 pp.

A review and evaluation of the first ten years of the BA (Publishing Studies) Course which has been offered at the Department of Book Industry at the University of Science and Technology in Kumasi since 1984. Sets out the aims and objectives of the programme, the teaching curriculum, staffing, and administration, followed by an analysis of graduates produced for the first decade, the placement of graduates, how they obtained jobs in the book industries, and an assessment of the performance of graduates on the jobs they now do. A final section looks at development plans for the Department until the year 2,000.

2557

Tita, Julius Che "Introducing Publishing Studies into University Education in Cameroon." *African Publishing Review* 4, no. 6 (November/December 1995): 12.

A brief account about a publishing course offered at the University of Buea in Cameroon, its present status and possible future development.

Zimbabwe International Book Fair

2558

Adeniyi, Dapo "Tantenda Zimbabwe." *Glendora Review* 1, no. 4 (1996): 11-16.

A report about the 1996 Zimbabwe International Book Fair, and about some the meetings and special events which coincided with the Fair, including a workshop for African journal editors, at which the writer (who is Editor of the *Glendora Review. African Quarterly of the Arts*) was one of the participants.

2559

Alexander, Ute "The Zimbabwe International Book Fair 1996." *Writers World*, no. 17 (October 1996): 16.

A South African poet writes about her visit to ZIBF 96 and the writers' workshop that was held during the Fair.

2560

Anon. *Zimbabwe International Book Fair. Catalogue 1996.* Harare: Zimbabwe International Book Fair Trust, 1996. 78 pp.

Official book fair catalogue and programme of associated events. Includes a complete listing of exhibitors by country which short profiles of exhibitors, and full contact information.

2561

Badisang, Bobana "Report on the Zimbabwe International Book Fair, Harare." *African Research & Documentation*, no. 70 (1996): 69-71.

Reports about the 1996 Zimbabwe Book Fair and about a number of meetings and workshops held during the Fair including one on the acquisitions of African-published materials by African libraries. Argues that some of the suggestions put forward at the workshops which might improve the acquisitions of African books are impractical, and suggests that APNET should have a permanent showroom, and should become a stock-holding operation to process libraries' orders from a central distribution point.

2562
Bond, Frances "Experiencing the Zimbabwean Bookfair." *Writers' World*, no. 13 (1994): 15-16.
    The author, a South African literary agent, was part of a group of South African delegates to the 1995 Zimbabwe International Book Fair, and found it an exciting experience.

2563
Cochran, Christopher Lee "Freedom of Expression-at the Zimbabwe Book Fair." *Information Development* 12, no. 2 (June 1996): 74.
    States that the article by Brenda Mitchell-Powell (see entry 2568 below) was marred by "a selective oversight by the author" by leaving out some vital reporting of important events that occurred during the Fair, namely the banning of the Gay and Lesbian's organization of Zimbabwe from exhibiting at the Fair, and the vitriolic attack on gays by President Mugabe, which made a mockery of the Fair's theme of 'Human rights and justice'.

2564
Dunton, Chris, and Mai Palmberg *Human Rights and Homosexuality in Southern Africa*. Uppsala: Nordiska Afrikainstitutet (Current African Issues, 19), 1996. 41 pp.
    At the 1997 Zimbabwe International Book Fair one of the exhibitors, the organization of Gays and Lesbians in Zimbabwe (GALZ), were prevented from taking part on the orders of the Zimbabwean government. This opened up an unprecedented, vigorous, and sometimes agonising debate in Southern Africa. The debate on these and other issues is conveyed in this report on the book fair drama in Zimbabwe, and the debates that followed in Botswana, Namibia and South Africa.

2565
Ling, Margaret "Minding the Business at ZIBF 96." *Bellagio Publishing Network Newsletter*, no. 18 (1996): 2-3.
    Evaluates the success of the 1996 ZIBF and provides some statistical analysis of exhibitor participation. The author directs the Zimbabwe International Book Fair's European office.

2566
Mbanga, Trish "The Zimbabwe International Book Fair: where to now?" *African Publishing Review* 5, no. 2 (March/April 1996): 6-7.
    Trish Mbanga, Director of ZIBF, in conversation with Lesley Humphrey, looks back over the past five years of the Fair and discusses some of its future plans.

2567
Mitchell-Powell, Brenda "Booksellers, Librarians Celebrate African Literature at ZIBF'95." *American Libraries* 26, no. 9 (October 1995): 880-882.
    An American librarian reports about her visit to the 1995 Zimbabwe International Book Fair, and the various special events and activities that coincided with the Fair. Also offers some observations on library services in the region, and finds that "on a continent overwhelmed with subsistence survival, African librarians face awesome challenges."

2568

Mitchell-Powell, Brenda   "The Zimbabwe International Book Fair 1995." *Information Development* 12, no. 1 (March 1996): 33-37.

> A further account about ZIBF 95 by this American librarian, including the pre-Fair meeting on 'Freedom of Expression' which was attended by several prominent African writers. Also provides some information about the African Publishers' Network and the African Periodicals Exhibit.

2569

Ranger, Terence. "Zimbabwe Book Fair: Controversy in 1995." *Bellagio Publishing Network Newsletter*, no. 15 (November 1995): 1-2.

> About the widely condemned exclusion of the Gay and Lesbians of Zimbabwe (GALZ) from exhibiting at the 1995 Zimbabwe International Book Fair. Although the ZIBF organizers had offered and allocated a booth to GALZ they were compelled at the last minute to withdraw exhibit facilities under a directive from the Zimbabwe Government Director of Information. This was followed by a hostile attack on gays by President Mugabe during his speech at the opening of the Fair.

2570

Treffgarne, Carew "1996 Zimbabwe International Book Fair." *ADEA Newsletter* 8, no. 4 (October-November 1996): 14.

> Looks back at the 1996 Zimbabwe Book Fair, and reports about the collaboration between the Fair organizers and the Association for the Development of Education in Africa's Working Group on Books and Learning Materials in sponsoring an 'Indaba' on national book policies. (see entry 2501 for 'Indaba' proceedings).

2571

Umbina, Anna "Time Warp." *The Zimbabwean Review* 2, no. 4 (October-December 1996): 28

> Describes the attempts to silence the Gay and Lesbians of Zimbabwe (GALZ) at the 1996 Zimbabwe Book Fair, which, for the second year running, was once again overshadowed by issues of human rights and freedom of expression.

Indexes

Author index

Murray, Steve   2493

Nassimbeni, Mary   2376
Newton, Diana   2310, 2418, 2505
Ngeze, Pius B.   2458
Nigerian Publishers Association   2280,
      2445
Njoku, N.A.   2509
Nnana-Rejasef, Marie-Claire   2323
Noma Award Managing Committee
      2506
Nwabera, Alice   2546
Nwafor, B.V.   2491
Nwankwo, Victor   2361, 2502, 2533
Nyamangara, William   2510
Nyambura, Joyce   2547

Odiadi, Austin   2511
Odufua, Tunde   2512
Ofei, Eric   2339
Ofori-Mensah, Akoss   2478
Ogolla, James   2437
Ogunleye, Bisi   2364
Okia, Martin   2274
Okoye, Ifeoma   2453, 2454
Okwilagwe, Andrew Oshiotse   2366
Olajide, Akin   2362
Olaniowo, Wale   2363
Olden, Anthony   2314, 2315
Oliphant, Andries Walter   2377
Olude, O.O.   2365
Omotoso, Kole   2503
Omowunmi, Segun   2455
Orimalade, Oluronke   2419, 2444
Osanyin, Bode   2521
Osborn, Paul   2505
Oshunfowora, Ranti E.   2287

Palmberg, Mai   2564
Palmeri, Robert J.   2331
Paradza, Vonai   2438
Philipparts, Michel   2311
Pinfold, John   2391
Potgieter, Alida   2456
Priestley, Carol   2420, 2504

Publishers' Association of South Africa
      2284
Pugliese, Cristiana   2289, 2399

Radebe, Thuli   2522
Randall, Isobel   2457
Randle, Ian   2296, 2439
Ranger, Terence   2569
Raseroka, H.K.   2392
Read, Tony   2332
Reece, Jane   2328
Reproduction Rights Organization of
      Kenya, The   2464
Reuster-Jahn, Uta   2400
Ripken, Peter   2409
Roberts, Frances   2285
Rosenberg, Diana   2421, 2422
Rowbotham, Graham   2420
Rudolph, John-Willy   2463
Russell, Terry   2493

Sagna, R.   2523
Salahi, Katherine   2411
Saro-Wiwa, Ken   2367
Shaba, Steve   2548
Sharples, Carolyn   2423
Shoyinka, S.A.   2515
Simwinga, Gideon   2386
Singh, Tejeshwar   2534
Southern African Book Development
      Education Trust   2286
Sow, Mamadou Aliou   2269
Staunton, Irene   2524
Sylla, Ibrahima   2324

Taylor, Ian   2424
Taylor, Sally   2378
Teferra, Damtew   2268, 2487, 2551
Tettey, Edem   2556
Thomas, Akin   2425
Thomas, Ruth   2488
Thumbadoo, Beulah   2271
Tita, Julius Che   2557
Treffgarne, Carew   2504, 2570
Tumusiime, James   2384

Geographical index

→   *Note:* Reference numbers in **bold** refer to entries in main sections
Parts 2 & 3

Africa (General studies) **2297-2312,**
2475, 2491

Africa, East **2313-2315**

Africa, Francophone 2269, 2272, 2310,
2316-2324, 2430, 2466, 2468, 2471,
2523, 2540

Africa, West **2325,** 2556

Africa, Southern **2326-2328,** 2391,
2461

Benin 2316, **2329-2330,** 2459, 2485

Botswana 2392

Cameroun 2486, 2557

Côte d'Ivoire 2316, **2331**

Eritrea **2332**

Ethiopia **2333-2334,** 2549

Ghana **2335-2339,** 2427, 2431, 2432,
2446, 2478, 2556

Kenya 2289, 2305, **2340-2346,** 2396,
2399, 2416, 2437, 2451, 2464, 2513,
2538, 2542, 2544

Lesotho 2461

Malawi **2347-2348**

Mali 2496, 2505

Namibia 2279

Nigeria 2280, 2287, **2349-2367,** 2404-
2406, 2408, 2410, 2412, 2415, 2425,
2443-2445, 2449, 2453, 2454, 2479,
2482, 2494, 2499, 2502, 2509, 2511,
2512, 2515, 2521, 2525, 2536, 2537,
2539, 2537, 2548

Senegal 2535

South Africa 2271, 2273, 2284, 2285,
2290, **2368-2379,** 2428, 2450, 2456,
2457, 2484, 2497, 2500, 2518, 2522

Swaziland 2461

Tanzania **2380,** 2400, 2452, 2458, 2467

Togo **2381,** 2397

Uganda 2274, **2382-2384,** 2479

Zambia **2385-2386,** 2470, 2476, 2477

Zimbabwe **2387,** 2395, 2398, 2414,
2434, 2441, 2493, 2510, 2524

Subject index

→ *Note:* Reference numbers in **bold** refer to entries in main sections Parts 1, 2 & 4